Finding the Nuts on the Family Tree

A guide for beginning researchers

Christine Sutton Dip. Family History

CHRIS SUTTON
DIP. FAMILY HISTORY

Christine Sutton has been a genealogist and family historian for over thirty years. She holds a Diploma in Family History from the University of Tasmania and qualifications in Education from several universities. With a background in writing, teaching, learning design and course development for all ages, she has a strong commitment to lifelong learning. Now retired, she spends much of her time sharing what she has learned with those beginning their journey into the family heritage.

Chris has produced a series of family history stories, workbooks, and case studies in Family History. She continues her own lifelong learning jouney with studies in history, writing and publishing through the Australian Open University and the UK's FutureLearn.

Chris lives in Beachmere, Queensland with her partner and their crazy labradoodle Nicnak Tiger Woods.

Her Mantra?

"It's not the family tree that's fascinating, it's the nuts that fall out of it."

CHRIS SUTTON'S BOOKS ARE AVAILABLE BY CONTACTING HER AT;

EMAIL: MCSUTTON@CHRIS-SUTTON.COM.AU

WEB: HTTPS://WWW.MCSUTTON.CHRIS-SUTTON.COM.AU

CONTENTS

FAMILY HISTORY

Family History is precisely that, the story of a family through history. Hundreds of thousands of people around the globe are engaged in tracing their family root for many reasons, all of which are right for them.

Here are a few of the most popular:

- ⅋ To satisfy their curiosity about themselves and their roots.
- ⅋ To provide their children with a sense of who their ancestors were, where they came from and how they lived their lives.
- ⅋ To preserve family cultural and ethnic traditions for future generations
- ⅋ To compile a medical family history to give family members an advantage in the battle against inherited diseases or defects.
- ⅋ To qualify for a lineage or heritage society.
- ⅋ To assemble and publish a family history book, whether for family members or for profit.
- ⅋ To discover facts that others have overlooked and to solve the puzzle of a lifetime.

Family historians want to know who their ancestors were, where, when and how they lived, what they did and why they did it. They look at a name on their family tree and wonder what that person was like. Were they respected? Was he/she an ordinary person or someone special?

If he/she was a convict, what was their crime, but why did they turn to crime? After their time in jail was over, did the convict live a law-abiding, useful life? How? With whom?

We're a nosy lot!

Why do we do this? For most of us, it is a desire to know where we came from; how we came to be the person we are. We want to know the people who passed on their genes, appearance, personality and values to us.

If we know where we have come from, we know better where we are going.

4

WHAT IS THE DIFFERENCE BETWEEN GENEALOGY AND FAMILY HISTORY?

The Oxford dictionary defines genealogy as *"A line of descent traced continuously from an ancestor."*

Traditionally, Genealogists use vital records and sound documentary evidence to trace back in a direct line from a single individual to their earliest recorded ancestor. The usual recording device is a Family Tree. The emphasis is often on how many generations there are on the tree, how high it has grown, and how many branches there are, how wide it spreads. They focus primarily on births, deaths, and marriages - names and dates.

Family historians take a different approach. They focus on the people, the fruit of the tree. They are interested in who their ancestors are, where they lived, how they lived and why they made their life choices. They are looking for the answers to what has made us the people we are today. It is the driving force behind the popular television series "Who Do You Think You Are?"

Neither of these approaches can stand alone.

Family historians need to practice correct genealogical research. They need to follow the basic principles of genealogical research to find the fruit of their tree and examine it. Family History brings another dimension to Genealogy. It enriches it.

As we set off in search of the family members who lived in the past, we find that they lived in an environment very different to ours. Their homes, their clothes and their surrounding objects, were of the technology of the time. They had different jobs, using different tools. While they may have lived in the same town, their homes, furniture, appliances and way of life were vastly different to ours.

Family Historians use historical times, photos, objects and places to better understand how and why their ancestors lived where they lived, worked as they worked, played as they played and how their environment affected their lives, and ultimately their descendants' lives.

FAMILY TREES

Over the centuries, genealogists have used Family Tree charts to record the ancestors (or descendants) of a particular person in a direct line.

If you record your forebears on a family tree backwards through the generations from a single individual, it is called an Ancestor Tree. Think of an ancestor tree as being in the shape of an upside-down triangle, a pyramid. The person who is the subject of the tree is at the bottom. Not counting second marriages, an individual will usually have two parents, four grandparents, eight great-grandparents, sixteen great-great-grandparents and so on.

If this is your tree, working upward from you, it forms your ancestral pyramid.

By the time you have gone back ten generations, you have an impressive 1,024 ancestors - more than enough to keep you busy researching for a lifetime!

Chart 1 is always the Master Ancestor Tree.

Keep adding ancestors and numbering accordingly. Then when you create an individual tree for any of your individual ancestors, note on their tree the number that is allocated to him/her on the main Ancestor Tree.

It sounds complicated, but it isn't, really. Just sketch one out on scrap paper and try it, or scan and print two copies of the Ancestor Tree form from the appendix and practice. You'll get the hang of it.

Chart 1
Ancestor Tree - Mary Christine AMBLER

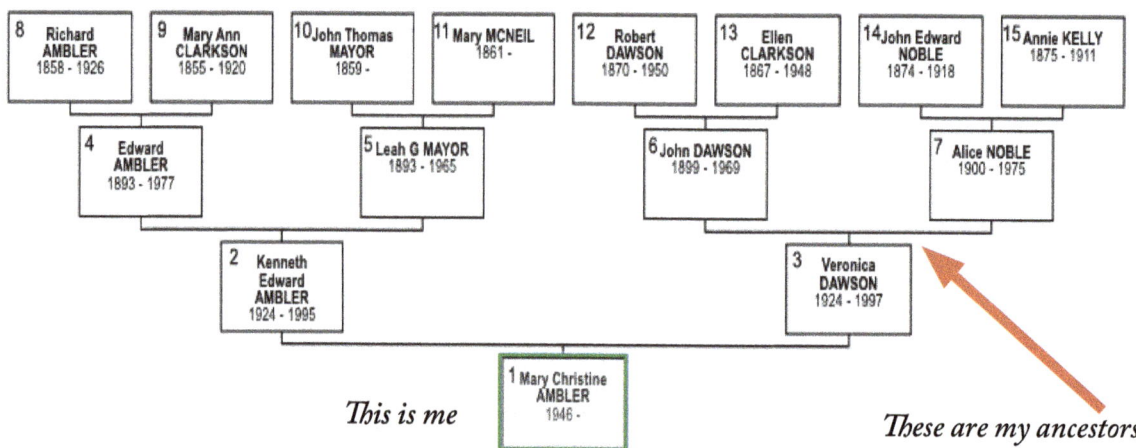

This is me

These are my ancestors

NOTE: Each person has a number, starting with the person who is the subject of the tree. On my family tree, I am number 1.

My parents are 2 and 3, male first, then female.

My grandparents are 4 & 5 (Paternal) 6 & 7 (Maternal) This numbering system continues for each person on the tree.

If another tree is started, for example, Richard Ambler's Ancestor Tree, I would label it *Chart 2: Ancestor Tree - Richard Ambler*. He would be person 1 on Chart 2. I would make a note in the top right corner that says *"Person 1 on this tree is Person 8 on Chart 1."* I would then file Chart 1 in my folder and Chart 2 in Richard Ambler's folder.

Descendants Tree

If you take this pyramid and turn it right-side-up, you are now at the top. Stretching down from you are your descendants- your children, grandchildren, great-grandchildren and so on. If you trace your family tree down from a single ancestor, then it is called a **descendant tree.**

Descendant Tree - Mary Christine AMBLER

This is Me

```
┌─────────────────┬─────────────────┐
│ Mary Christine  │ Robert John     │
│ AMBLER          │ SUTTON          │
│ 1946 -          │ 1944 - 2010     │
└─────────────────┴─────────────────┘

┌──────────┬──────────┐   ┌──────────┬──────────┬──────────┐
│ Timothy  │ Catherine│   │ Michael  │ Scott    │ Tracey   │
│ John     │ DORLING  │   │ Peter    │ Edward   │ Lee      │
│ SUTTON   │          │   │ SUTTON   │ SUTTON   │ EVANS    │
│ 1967 -   │ 1969 -   │   │ 1969 -   │ 1972 -   │ 1972 -   │
└──────────┴──────────┘   └──────────┴──────────┴──────────┘

┌──────────┬──────────┐   ┌──────────┬──────────┬──────────┬──────────┐
│ Genevieve│ Charlotte│   │ Zachary  │ Morgyn   │ Caleb    │ Makaylie │
│ SUTTON   │ SUTTON   │   │ Scott    │ JONES    │ SUTTON   │ SUTTON   │
│ 1997 -   │ 2002 -   │   │ SUTTON   │          │ 1996 -   │ 2001 -   │
│          │          │   │ 1990 -   │          │          │          │
└──────────┴──────────┘   └──────────┴──────────┴──────────┴──────────┘

                          ┌──────────┐
                          │ Freya Joy│
                          │ SUTTON   │
                          │ 2017 -   │
                          └──────────┘
```

This is my youngest descendant

There are some conventions that are used on all family trees;

- ℘ Surnames should be in upper case, e.g. SUTTON and Given names in normal case e.g. Robert. Parents should be entered with father to the left and mother to the right.
- ℘ Women are always entered with their surname at birth (maiden name)
- ℘ If a date of birth or death is not known you may leave it blank, or if you have an approximate year enter is as C (Circa) or Abt (about), e.g. C1865 or Abt 1865

In the next Section we look at the process of finding and verifying the evidence that we use to make entries on the Family Tree.

THE FAMILY DETECTIVE

Family history is not an exact science. Absolute proof is not always possible to find. At best, we can make an educated guess supported by strong evidence from a variety of sources.

To establish the identity of a person and their relationship to ourself, it is necessary to find documentary or primary source evidence.

The Oxford Dictionary defines evidence as;

> *"Information drawn from personal testimony, a document, or a material object, used to establish facts..."*

Family History research is detective work. We sift through miles of paperwork, troll the Internet and pester relatives for information.

We interview and record stories, examine photographs and old objects, and pore over maps. We do all this to establish the facts of our heritage and to prove we are who we think we are.

The most usual form of evidence is a birth, marriage or death certificate. We call these "vital records". However, family historians may find other evidence in family bibles, church records or census returns and electoral roles.

Searching from the present and going back four generations can be relatively easy.

Compulsory registration of births started in the mid-19th century. The collective family memory provides many clues to where you might look. Letters and diaries may still exist, old address books lie in boxes under beds.

The further back in time we go, the harder it is to find evidence. For example, prior to 1750, many churches were destroyed in times of religious persecution, civil war and rebellion, together with their records. Therefore, church records of baptisms, banns, marriages, and burials are more difficult to find.

Yet there are exceptions. Scottish Church records, for example, have survived exceptionally well. They are invaluable and cover a longer period and a wider scope. For example, episcopalian church communion rolls are a kind of church membership record and can provide information as to a profession, employment, and/or place of origin.

You will meet brick walls, but persistence pays off, and many years down the track you might come across that piece of the jigsaw that solves your 'cold case'.

For example, my grandmother was told by her parents that her brother died in a gangland killing in the USA in 1920.

To date, we could not find a death certificate. However, what we have found is an application for citizenship completed in 1925 with a signature that matches his British Army recruitment papers and pension records, together with a draft card from 1942, again with a matching signature.

We have a solid basis to say that these records were his. On both these records, it describes him as having a glass eye.

Uncle Robbie lost an eye in 1918 while working as a riveter in the Glasgow Dockyards.

An educated guess, supported by this evidence, leads us to believe that my great grandparents probably lied to their daughters.

However, we can only say that it is most likely that Robert Andrew Mayor did not die in 1920.

We have no proof of this, yet.

BASIC PRINCIPLES

To discover and understand the ancestors who passed on their family traits, including appearance, personality, and values, we need to turn first to the Basic Principles of Genealogical Research. Along the way, we can take pride in our ancestors' achievements and ensure that those who come after us know their heritage and why we, as a family, are the way we are.

PRINCIPLE 1 - MOVE FROM THE KNOWN TO THE UNKNOWN, FROM THE PRESENT TO THE PAST.

In Family History, as in all research, we move from the known to the unknown. Known really means KNOWN. There needs to be evidence that what you think you know is really the way it truthfully is. You need as many vital records (birth, marriage, death) as you can find for your immediate family group.

Dig out those birth certificates for you, your parents and any other current family members. Record the information you already know,

- ❧ Names,
- ❧ Dates,
- ❧ Places.

Decide what you want to find out. Do you want to investigate some old family stories that you heard from your grandparents or solve a family mystery? Whatever it is, you need to apply the skills of a detective to track back from the now to the past. Your trail will lead from today, backwards in time from you to your parents, then grandparents, then great grandparents until you find the person you are searching for.

PRINCIPLE 2 - DON'T MAKE ANY ASSUMPTIONS.

Everything is only speculation until we verify it. Start with yourself and work backwards, proving each step as you go. It is important that you talk to members of your family, particularly the older ones. So often I have heard family historians say,

'I should have spoken to Grandma or Grandad - but it is too late now.'

Find the custodian of your family's history and pick their brains. Search for old letters, diaries, photographs, certificates — in fact, anything you can find which might bear on your family history research. You never know what you might find. My mother-in-law had a family bible, on the middle page of which I found the signatures and details of all of her brothers and sisters who had signed the temperance pledge, some of whom no-one had ever mentioned.

- ❧ Share your information. You never know who might have the missing piece of the family jigsaw puzzle. Many years ago, long before the Internet, a genealogist in Nottingham contacted me after I had advertised my research interests through the Genealogical Society in Sydney. We were searching the same mass migration of British Lace workers from Nottingham to Calais in the 1700s. These lace workers made a second migration to South Australia and NSW. The outcome of sharing our research with other researchers was the formation of the Society of the Lace makers of Calais.

- ❧ Know that family myths are a great trap for beginners. Our myth was that the Lovetts came to England from Normandy in 1066 with William the Conqueror. I ignored it, started my ancestor chart at Robert, working backwards. I can get back to 1796. No older records are available. Between 1066 and 1796 there is a big gap in the records and hence the family tree!

PRINCIPLE 3 - CHECK THE SPELLING

The spelling of names varies. It isn't true to say that "it's not my family because we don't spell our name that way". When many people could not read or write, authorities had to write everything for them. People wrote what they heard. For example, MacNeil and McNeil were different spellings of the same name.

Variations in pronunciation also led to different spellings of the same name: a person from the north of England might have pronounced a name differently to someone from Ireland. My Brogans were from Ireland, and one spelling I came across was B-r-o-a-d-e-n (Broaden). If you listen carefully, you can hear the Irish accent.

Human characteristics also created spelling variations: for example, a person with a lisp might pronounce the 's' sound differently and so the spelling might reflect this.

Then there is the 'Hyacinth Bucket/Hyacinth Bouquet' factor. Pretensions to grandeur may result in different spellings: Smith transformed into Smythe, Brown with an 'e' added, and so on.

Many people anglicised their names; Muller became Miller, Ah Kin became King. Indexers transcribed records and information wrongly. I couldn't find my grandmother's death record. They indexed her as Dawfon instead of Dawson. Why does this matter? Because you enter names on search forms. What you enter is what the computer will look for. On computer search forms, always tick the box for searches that include surname variations. Watch, also, for

- The interchanging of vowels — a, e, i, o, u and the silent consonant y
- If it starts with h, drop the h
- If it starts with a vowel, then add an h. The surnames Anderson and Henderson, for example, are often interchangeable in indexes. .

PRINCIPLE 4 - RECORDED AGES MAY NOT ALWAYS BE ACCURATE

Just because there is information recorded on a birth, death or marriage certificate, or in a book or newspaper or on an internet site, or even in Ancestry.com, does not mean it is true. Always check. Never assume the age is correct. Some people didn't know how old they were. Others saw advantages in 'adjusting' their age.

- Young men wanting to enlist, when they weren't old enough, adjusted their age or adopted the age of an older sibling. A good example of deliberate age change is that of an older woman lowering her age to better match that of a prospective husband.

- Many of our ancestors arrived under one migration scheme or another. There were rules and regulations and often strict age criteria. If all your family qualified, but you didn't, would your parents have left you behind or tinkered with your age so you could go too? Australian convict research reveals that ages could vary significantly. For example, they recorded 16 as the age of a female convict. Two weeks later, she said,

"I am an orphan. I have no parents. I do not know how old I am." She could have been any age.

PRINCIPLE 5 - KEEP GOOD RECORDS. GET ORGANISED.

Keep a careful record of your research. Use standard charts and a research log. Back up your research and document your sources. This gives integrity to your research and allows others to track where you have been. You might put down a search and pick it up again years later. It can frustrate you not to know where a particular document came from.

Getting organised

- Most family historians use the following charts;
- Family tree - Ancestor and/or Descendant
- Ancestor Chart for each person
- Family Group for each ancestor their spouse/s and their children
- Research log to record each search, the results, source, and citation.
- Source summary to record all sources cited.
- Correspondence log to keep track of everyone who sent you information and what they responded with.

Chart Conventions

- Capitalise surnames
- Always use a woman's maiden name.
- Write dates in full to prevent confusion.
- To a place name, add State/County, and Country
- Use the standard abbreviations for places. (Chapman Codes)

On the charts, men go on the top and the women on the bottom. Number the people on the charts.

If we start with you, then you are number one on this chart. Your dad is number 2 and your mum is number 3. Your paternal grandparents are 4 and 5, your maternal grandparents are 6 and 7, and so on.

NOTE: The Chapman Codes are the abbreviations we use every day to abbreviate the names of countries, states, counties and places. For example, New South Wales =NSW, West Australia =WA, United Kingdom = UK, United States of America =USA, Lancashire =LANCS. Do not mix them up with the country codes used on Internet web addresses. They are different. You can find a global list of Chapman Codes online on the Genealogical Society of Queensland website; *https://www.gsq.org.au/what-gsq-offers/resource-centre/gsq-call-number-system/chapman-codes/*

YOUR FILING SYSTEM

With all of these charts to keep in order your filing system becomes important. There are a variety of ways you can organise your physical records from colour based systems to organising by type and date of record and event. The main thing is to choose something that you'll use and stick to it. It's all too easy to have stacks of paper and boxes of unsorted photos lying about.

Like many genealogists, you may find yourself with primary documents, photographs and memorabilia passed down from previous generations and these (along with the images and documents you are currently creating) need to be preserved for the future. It's advisable to digitise them, where possible, to provide digital copies that can be shared with family members. This cuts down on handling the originals and gives you a backup in case the physical originals are destroyed by fire. Backup on USB sticks, or external hard drives and keep the backups in a separate place.

If you choose to file electronically, scanning all of the certificates becomes essential.

You need to keep all of the documents for an individual in a directory/folder for just that person. Then their directory goes inside their family group folder, which is inside the family folder and inside the Family Tree folder.

If you use specialised software, e.g. Family Tree Maker, your software will do this for you. However, the filing system is controlled by the software and has a different structure to the filing system on your computer's hard drive.

A word to the wise; Backup! Backup! Backup!

One day you **will** suffer a hard disk crash. It is inevitable. It will happen. You need to have a backup on another computer or a USB or external drive and preferably one 'in the cloud', that is, on Google Drive, Drop Box, Evernote or whatever cloud based backup service you choose. There is nothing more soul destroying that thousands of hours of research, documents, photos and other records lost forever.

If you prefer not to use computer technology, your hard copy or paper files are kept in much the same way.

- ❧ - A Family Tree filing cabinet
- ❧ - A drawer for each family tree if necessary
- ❧ - A hanger for each family in each drawer
- ❧ - A folder (or two, or three, or ...) in each hanger for each individual.

I prefer to use both systems. Inside each physical folder I have plastic wallets and sleeves for the original and a paper copy of each kind of document; certificates, newspaper clippings etc.

The disadvantage of a physical filing system is the chance of loss in case of fire or flood. Hence I keep both. At least if there is a fire, I have scans of all of the priceless photos and information stored off site.

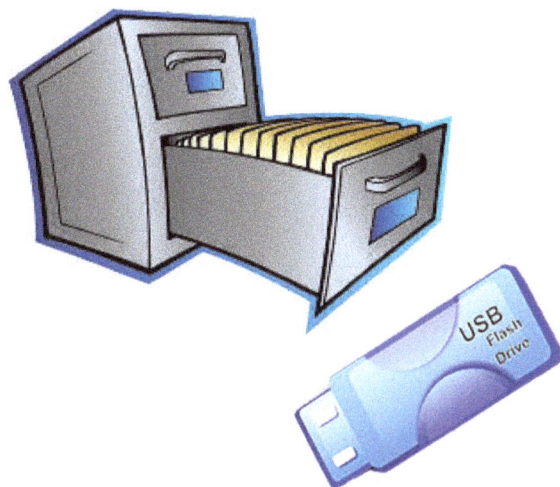

> *The past we explore and the people we seek are a fascinating spiral of false leads, confused identities, and tangled lives. As family historians, we inherit the job of unearthing every clue and weighing every fragment of evidence so carefully that we piece together an accurate mosaic of each ancestral life.*
>
> *Elizabeth Shown Mills*

The first important step in setting out on your family history journey is to write down what you already know. Choose one person to research at a time. If you try to research more than one you will become tangled up in who belongs to whom and who lived where. Start with yourself, then move on to one of your parents.

1. Start your filing system by using the charts provided in the appendix.
2. Write down what you already know about any new individual. This information might be from firsthand experience or documents you might have already collected.
3. Search for anything that might provide you with clues for your research. Look for copies of;
   - ᴥ Vital records (birth certificates, marriage certificates and death certificates)
   - ᴥ Family Bibles and diaries
   - ᴥ School reports
   - ᴥ Photographs and old letters
   - ᴥ Obituaries and wills
   - ᴥ Newspaper clippings

Resist the temptation to copy information from other people's trees. This may corrupt your research and you will end up with a spiders web of mis-information.

Use your ancestry or pedigree chart to record this information. This highlights what you need to locate or verify the gaps in your research. Next, decide what you want to find out. Break it down into simple questions;

- ᴥ What is the name of the person that you are researching?
- ᴥ When and where were they born? What did they look like?
- ᴥ If they married, where did they marry?
- ᴥ How many children did they have?

- ᴥ What were the names of their children?
- ᴥ Where did the person live?
- ᴥ What type of work did they do?
- ᴥ What religion and/or organisations did they belong to?
- ᴥ When and where did they die?
- ᴥ What was the cause of death?
- ᴥ Were they buried or were they cremated? If they were buried, where were they buried?
- ᴥ Did they have a headstone?

Taking one step at a time - one individual, one question, one task - consider the list of questions you have written down and tackle the first one.

For example, "When and where was this person born?"

- ᴥ Ask yourself where you might locate that particular record.
- ᴥ Is there an index online?
- ᴥ Are there any access requirements?
- ᴥ Will you need to provide ID?
- ᴥ Will there be a cost?
- ᴥ Is the actual record available online?

When you have found the likely source of the information, locate and obtain the record you need. It is not enough to locate the record in an index. You need to get a copy, or view a digital copy, of the original document. Remember to use available online Searching Aids to help you search any website you might use.

Examine the record for the information you are seeking – that is, look carefully at all the information on the record.

Look for clues for further research. What do you see on the record? Will it help you with further research?

As you evaluate the information you have found, ask:

  € Did I find the information I was looking for?

  € Is the information complete?

  € Does the information conflict with other information I have?

  € Is the source of the information credible?

Record any new information on your charts – always including the source of the information. This is especially important if you have conflicting information: the most reliable source – generally – is the one made closest to the event.

Have an Aim for Each Research Task

If you want to keep your family history costs down, it is vital to have an aim for your research.

Every time you sit down to research online, you should know what you are looking for and where you might find it. This not only saves time, it saves money. If you are paying for a subscription that is time bound, or costs you per view of an original document or index entry, each time you repeat the same search is wasting your precious time and costing you dollars. Keep a log of your searches and their results on the log form in the appendix..

Documenting your sources is always important. Place a note on anything that you record of where you found it. If there are citation details available on the source, record them. Ancestry, for example, provides citation details for all its sources.

Any statement of fact that is not common knowledge must carry its own individual statement of where you found it. Source notes have two purposes:

1. To record the specific location of each piece of information; and
2. To record details that might have an impact on your evaluation of that information.

By recording where you found information, you will always know where to find it again. Other researchers will also be able to track your research path. This gives integrity to your research.

WEIGH UP EACH PART OF THE EVIDENCE.

When researching your family history be critical of the information you have found. Do not accept it at face value.

  € You may find that information is not what you were expecting: spelling, place of birth of parents, the parents themselves, especially the father. Dates might not be what you expect.

  € If it is an original copy of a record, you might have difficulty reading it.

  € Think about how much processing the source material has undergone. Has the record been recopied, perhaps more than once? Each time a copy or transcription is made there is a risk of error. Always ask yourself "Is the document I have a copy of the original record or a copy of a copied original record?"

  € The purpose of a record and the motivation of its creators frequently affects its truthfulness – the obituary of one of a friend's ancestors makes him sound like an important self-made man and entrepreneur, a free immigrant, rather than the poor Irish convict he was.

  € Marriage records may be backdated to hide an illegitimate birth.

  € Diaries written for public viewing may add undeserved importance to the writer's role in an event.

  € The most reliable informants generally have firsthand knowledge of an event. *Consider how true the information is, and whether the informant is relying on hearsay.* The truthfulness and skill of a record's creator will have shaped its content.

  € Timeliness generally adds to a document's credibility – did months elapse between the event and the creation of the record that relates its details?

  € Never be satisfied with just one record about an event.

  € Beware relying on circumstantial evidence.

EVIDENCE

Family History research can never be completely evidence based. The recording of births, deaths and marriages for the general population only commenced during the Tudor dynasty and the establishment of the Church of England, when churches were required to keep records. While many of these have been preserved and some are digitised, there are also a great deal of church documents that have been destroyed by fire, natural disasters and war. Records prior to the mid-1800s, when registration at government level became compulsory, are inexact and subject to inaccuracies of spelling, transcription and reliability. Many of these early records have also have been destroyed by war and neglect. It is accepted that accurately identifying your ancestors is often a 'best guess' situation, provided that the 'best guess' is based on best practice and the use of reliable, valid, accurate and authoritative sources.

It is essential that, if available, the original documents are sighted and their identifying record numbers are recorded. Transcripts are not always accurate and reliable.

Accepting the results of someone else's research from a website such as Family Search or Ancestry is fraught with danger.

BIRTH & BAPTISMAL CERTIFICATES:

Prior to birth certificates, baptismal records were the primary source of birth records. A birth or baptismal certificate can tell you far more than simply the date of birth, names of parents, their occupation and place of abode. If you look deeper into the record you may find clues as to who this family really was, how they lived, the social environment that impacted on their lives and some of the issues and politics with which they had to deal.

....

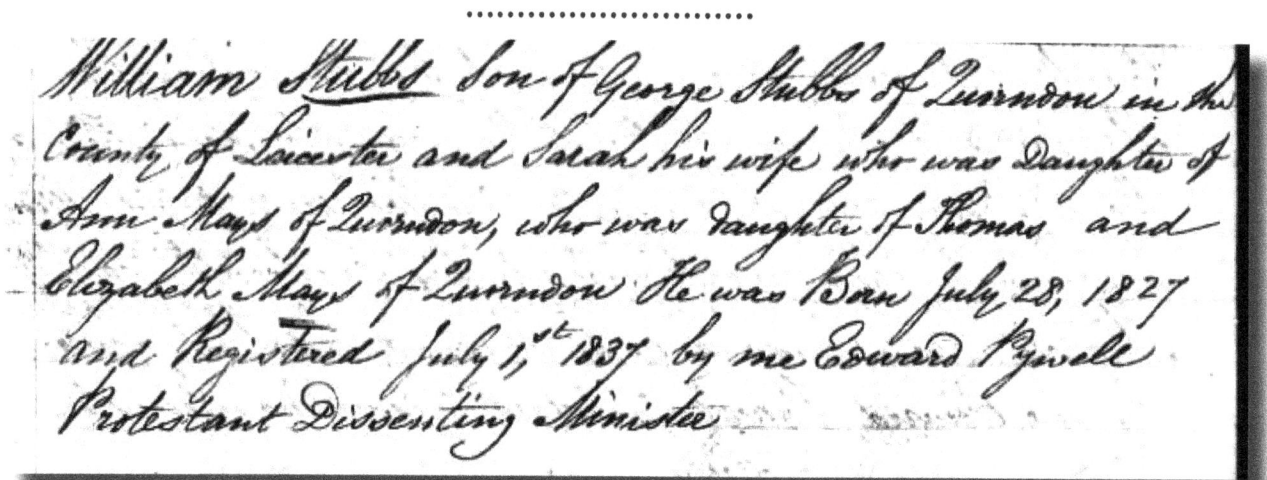

Transcript

"William Stubbs Son of Thomas Mays of Quorndon in the Parish of Barrow upon Soar in the County of Leicester, and Sarah his wife who was daughter Ann Mays of Quorndon who was daughter of Thomas and Elizabeth Mays of Quorndon. He was born July 28th 1827 and registered July 1st 1837 by me Edward Pywell Protestant Dissenting Minister"   (Note: There are ten years between birth and baptism)

This baptismal record from Quorndon in Leicestershire, England, is a goldmine. It gives the mother's name and grandmother's name and grandmother's parents names. "...Sarah, daughter of Ann Mays, who was daughter of Thomas and Elizabeth Mays..." It also reveals that the child was 1 year old when baptised and that his mother was illegitimate.

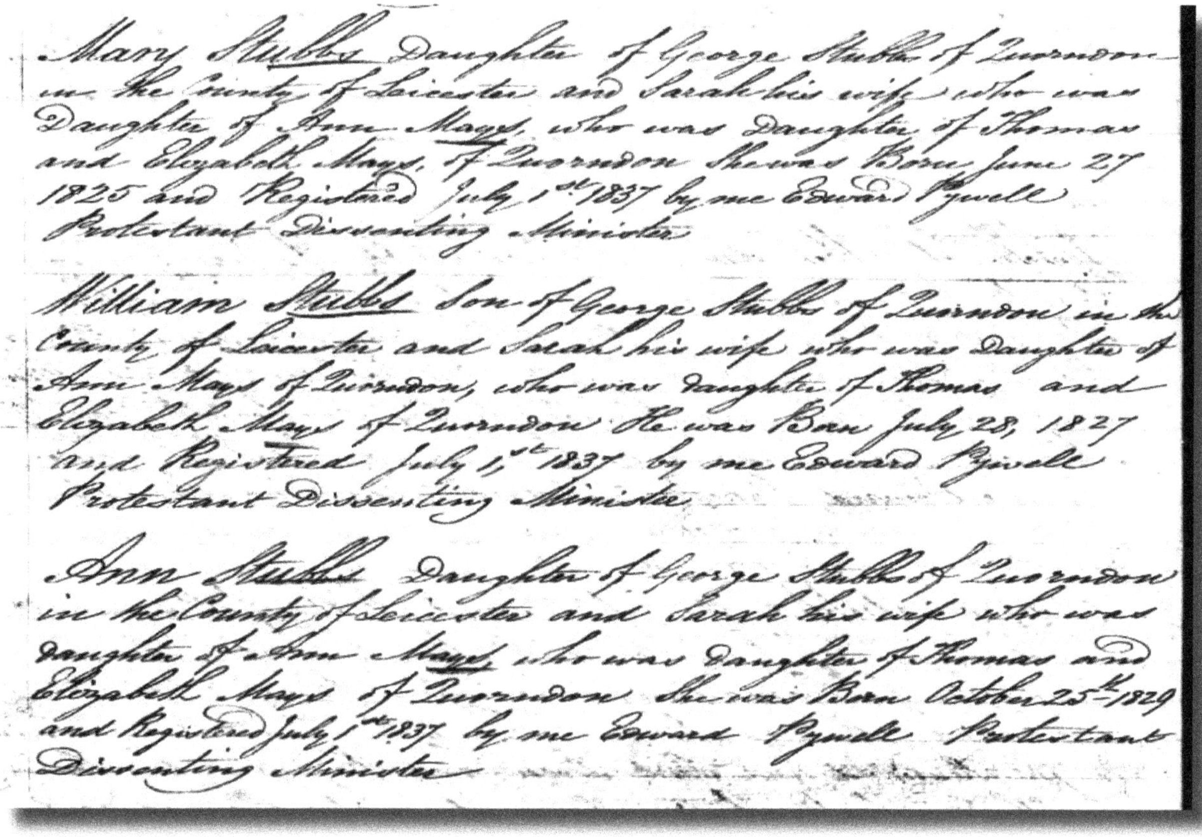

[Handwritten baptismal record: three entries in cursive script]

Mary Stubbs Daughter of George Stubbs of Quorndon in the County of Leicester and Sarah his wife who was Daughter of Ann Mays, who was Daughter of Thomas and Elizabeth Mays, of Quorndon She was Born June 27 1825 and Registered July 1st 1837 by me Edward Pywell Protestant Dissenting Minister

William Stubbs Son of George Stubbs of Quorndon in the County of Leicester and Sarah his wife who was Daughter of Ann Mays of Quorndon, who was daughter of Thomas and Elizabeth Mays of Quorndon He was Born July 28, 1827 and Registered July 1st 1837 by me Edward Pywell Protestant Dissenting Minister

Ann Stubbs Daughter of George Stubbs of Quorndon in the County of Leicester and Sarah his wife who was daughter of Ann Mays who was daughter of Thomas and Elizabeth Mays of Quorndon She was Born October 25th 1829 and Registered July 1st 1837 by me Edward Pywell Protestant Dissenting Minister

The family's religion is given as protestant dissenting. On the same page as this baptismal record are others from the same family. This may indicate that a dissenting church had been newly opened, or that they had not had a church within easy reach of their home and had travelled some distance for the baptism, or that the family were recent converts.

Dissenters were Protestants who had broken away from the Church of England, including Baptists, Methodists and Quakers, usually from the industrial and business communities. They suffered terrible persecution and discrimination in the 17th and 18th centuries.

William and his siblings would have been excluded from holding public office and education, they would not have been accepted into schools and University. Therefore, they would have attended schools set up by their Protestant community and had to go to Scottish University to obtain the degree of MD.

The Dissenters did not need acts of parliament to build their chapels.

The congregations funded their own buildings and ministers.

As a result, they could respond more readily to the growth of the towns and the migration of people from the countryside to the towns.

Among the Quakers there grew up several important business dynasties including the chocolate manufacturers such as Fry and Rowntree. Abraham Darby, the steel pioneer at Coalbrookdale, was also a Quaker.

The persecution suffered by the Dissenters contributed to mass overseas migrations of families from England to the colonies, including the lace workers of Leicester and Nottingham to France and later to Australia. William's family moved from Quorndon to Calais, France in the 1830s. The persecution experienced by dissenters may have been a factor in their looking for a place to live outside England, and also in their decision to emigrate to the colonies rather than return to England in 1842, when a world wide economic depression caused the lace industry and other textile manufacturing to falter.

MARRIAGE CERTIFICATES:

A marriage certificate provides information concerning the bride and groom; their occupation and address, their parents' names and father's occupation, the place married and their religion.

You may, on some certificates, find that if either party was underage, there are details of consent to the marriage.

If the date of the wedding is pre-registration and is a church record, there may also be records of marriage banns before the wedding. Traditionally banns were called on three consecutive occasions, usually at Sunday services, to allow anyone who objected to the marriage to come forward.

You may sometimes find marriage banns and not locate a marriage record. This may indicate that the marriage did not take place. However, it may also suggest a wedding in a different church or that the banns were considered to be the marriage. Never assume anything.

On the Marriage certificate opposite, note the signatures. Neither of the Pound siblings, Sarah nor her brother Jesse, could sign their names. They made a mark that needed to be witnessed by the other witness or the officiating minister. The father was a farmer. There may have been no schooling available. Here's an opportunity for further investigation. Could be a great family story!

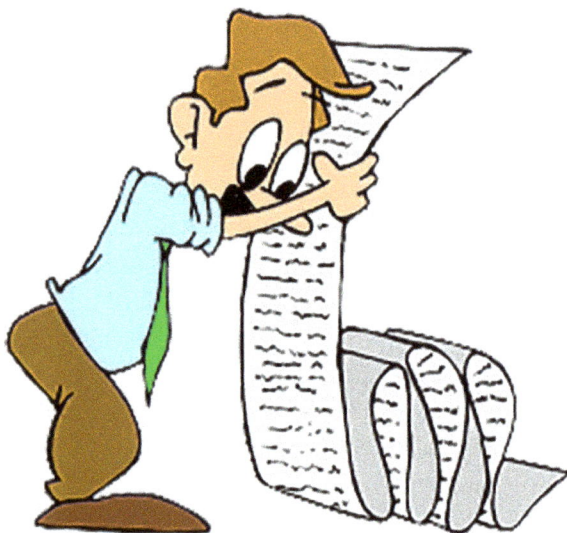

DEATH CERTIFICATES:

Death certificates are the richest source of information for Family Historians. Besides the name, address and date details you will find;

- Occupation
- Age at death
- Cause of death, length of illness and the name of the physician
- Name and occupation of father
- Maiden name and surname of mother
- Where buried
- How long in Australia
- When and where buried and the name of the undertaker
- Place of marriage, age and to whom
- All children living and deceased at the time of death and their ages
- Who informed authorities of the death

A word of caution, death certificates are sometimes hearsay records and may need to be treated as Secondary Sources of information. The certificate opposite is a vital record for the daughter of a convict. He died when she was a small child, and her mother was also deceased. The death was registered by a brother who would have been too young to remember his father. There are errors in the death certificate that could have sent the researcher off on false trails.

BIRTHS, DEATHS AND MARRIAGES AT SEA

If you suspect a death was at sea, search for a burial certificate or a record in the country of registration of the vessel.

The following is an online list of Marriages at sea from the Public Records Office. The Ships List

http://www.theshipslist.com/Forms/ marriagesatsea.html

People who married on the voyage to Australia may also be registered in the UK as married in 'Stepney'.

Transcript: Date and place of marriage 24th March 1875, Bathurst | **Names and Surnames of parties** James Lovett Sarah Pound| **Conjugal Status** Bachelor Spinster| **Birthplace** England N.S.Wales | **Usual Occupation** Storekeeper (None given for Sarah) | **Usual place of residence** Native Dog Creek Black Springs Swatchfield |**Father's Name, mother's name and maiden surname** William Lovett Sarah Wallace James Pound Hannah Surrey | **Father's Occupation** Carpenter Farmer | **Married in** St Stephen's Church Bathurst **According to the Rights** of the Presbyterian Church | **The Marriage was between us** James Lovett (signed) Sarah Pound (her mark)| **In the Presence of us** Jane Lovett (signature) Jesse Pound (His Mark)| **by** A Constable Gookie Officiating Minister.

Death Certificate of Ann Rebecca Collins.

There are a number of omissions and errors in this certificate that could provide a trap for the unwary.

The name of her father was unknown. He had died when she was a small child. She would have had little knowledge of him and therefore the registrant, her son-in-law , would have had little knowledge of the details of Anne's parentage and history.

The details of these taken from other primary sources were;

Name and Occupation of father - Edmund Collins, convict - later baker and confectioner and at time of death, miner.

Mothers name and maiden name - Catherine Brogan

In addition to these omissions and errors, the second child's name (he was always known as Ned) was Edmond, not Edward.

While a goldmine of information, double check every fact with the other vital records for each person to whom they refer, e.g. find Anne's birth certificate and confirm her parentage with *evidence.*

LET'S GET STARTED

Remember, Principle 1 is 'Start with the known'. The member of your family that you know the most about is yourself. Gather together all of the vital records that you have for yourself. Here's a checklist of what you need. If you aren't married, don't worry about it yet. You aren't dead, so there's not a death certificate on the list.

Vital records:

Birth Certificate ❑

Marriage Certificate ❑

Church records:

Baptismal Certificate ❑

On the page opposite record the facts from those vital records. Only record the information that is there, no family myths, no 'I remember' information, just the recorded facts. These are the details you will transfer to your Ancestor Chart, using 1 for your number on the chart.

Now find the information you have for your parents and grandparents. If there is none, ask your relatives for copies of any original vital records they may have, send for copies from the registrar's office for any that cannot be found.

Vital records:

Birth Certificate ❑

Marriage Certificate ❑

Death Certificate ❑

Church records:

Baptismal Certificate ❑

Burial Certificate ❑

Now record the information from your parents' vital records. Do not worry about your brothers and sisters yet. Enter your parents' details on the page opposite. Again, make sure you use details only from the original records. If there is information that you do not have, leave it empty for now. This will be your first piece of research - finding the missing pieces in the puzzle.

YOU

First Name_____

Middle Name _____

Last Name (UPPER CASE) _____

Birth Date _____   Location _____

Spouse First Name _____

      Last Name (UPPER CASE) _____

Marriage Date _____ Location_____

YOUR FATHER

First Name_____

Middle Name _____

Last Name (UPPER CASE) _____

Birth Date _____   Location _____

Spouse First Name _____

      Last Name (UPPER CASE) _____

Marriage Date _____ Location_____

Death Date _____   Location _____

YOUR MOTHER

First Name_____

Middle Name _____

Last Name (UPPER CASE) _____

Birth Date _____   Location _____

Spouse First Name _____

      Last Name (UPPER CASE)_____

Marriage Date _____ Location_____

Death Date _____   Location _____

Do the same thing for your grandparents. Transcribe their details into the form below. Transfer them to the family tree numbering your father's parents, 4 and 5; your mother's parents 6 and 7. Your family tree now has three generations on it. If you have used copies of the full vital records, your research has a sound base to work from.

YOUR FATHER'S FATHER

First Name_____

Middle Name _____

Last Name (UPPER CASE) _____

Birth Date _____   Location _____

Spouse First Name _____

       Last Name (UPPER CASE)_____

Marriage Date _____   Location_____

Death Date _____   Location _____

YOUR FATHER'S MOTHER

First Name_____

Middle Name _____

Last Name (UPPER CASE) _____

Birth Date _____   Location _____

Spouse First Name _____

       Last Name (UPPER CASE) _____

Marriage Date _____   Location_____

Death Date _____   Location _____

YOUR MOTHER'S FATHER

First Name _____

Middle Name _____

Last Name (UPPER CASE) _____

Birth Date _____ Location_____

Spouse First Name _____

          Last Name (UPPER CASE) _____

Marriage Date _____ Location _____

Death Date _____ Location _____

YOUR MOTHER'S MOTHER

First Name _____

Middle Name _____

Last Name (UPPER CASE) _____

Birth Date _____ Location_____

Spouse First Name _____

          Last Name (UPPER CASE) _____

Marriage Date _____ Location _____

Death Date _____ Location _____

As you keep adding generations your tree will get wider and wider.

Stick to parents until you become very good at building your tree, and more importantly, reading it!.

Stick to one family for a while, either your father's ancestors or your mother's.

Later you can start adding siblings (brothers and sisters). Soon your family tree will start to grow.

This is just a fraction of one side of my children's family tree.

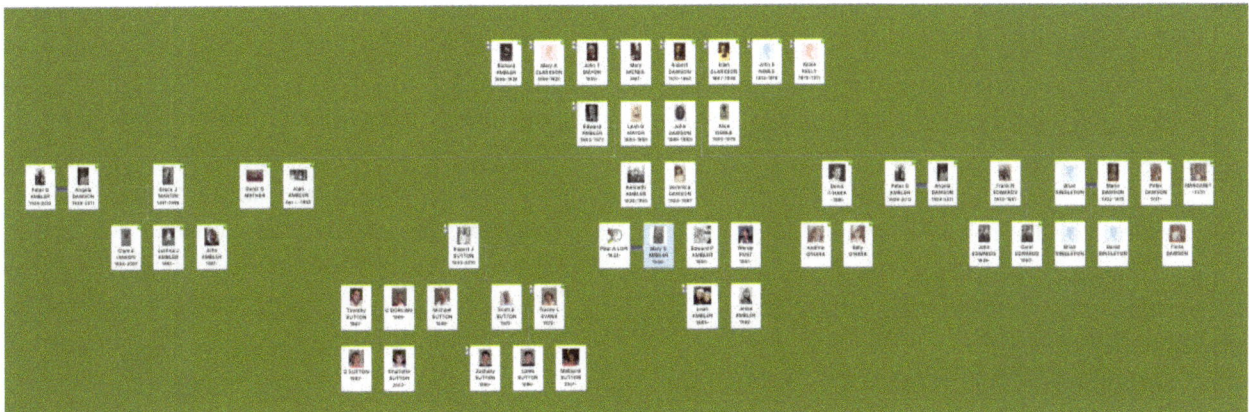

RELATIONSHIPS

There are several types of charts to help you determine family relationships. However, you will often find descriptions of family relationships in documents. You need to know to what the terminology actually refers. The meaning of the word "cousin," along with the meanings of other relationship terms, have changed over time.

1. *Lineal relationships* Are the relationship between you and your ancestors and descendants. They are very straightforward, (pardon the pun) or straight backwards. Sometimes the family tree entries in your software or online service will show a relationship. They may say 2x great grandfather of Mary Christine Ambler, or 2nd great grandfather. This means that the person is your great-grandfather's father, your great-great-grandfather. It makes it easier to say when you get to your 4th great-grandfather.

2. *Cousins* You will hear people say "He's my third cousin, once removed". We don't think about our relationships in such terms. 'Cousin' seems good enough. When working on your family history, however, it's more important to understand the various types of cousin relationships.

   &. First cousins are the people in your family who have two of the same grandparents as you.

   &. Second cousins have the same great-grandparents as you, but not the same grandparents.

   &. Third cousins have in common two great-great-grandparents and their ancestors.

When cousins descend from common ancestors by a different number of generations they are called 'removed'.

Once removed means there is a difference of one generation. Your mother's first cousin is one generation younger than your grandparents and you are two generations younger than your grandparents.

Your mother's first cousin is your first cousin,

once removed.

Twice removed means that there is a two-generation difference.

Confusing? After a while you get the hang of it.

3. *Half Relationships* exist between individuals who have a common ancestor but descend from different spouses of that ancestor. For example, half-brothers or sisters may have the same father but different mothers or the same mother but different fathers. The children of these half-siblings would be your half-cousins, because they share only one of the grandparents. Half-relationships are still considered consanguineous (blood) relationships along the line which the two individuals share.

4. *Step Relationships* (including "in-law" relationships) are relationships which occur through marriage. Your relationships with your step-relatives are not consanguineous as they are only related to you through marriage, not blood. They are not considered a part of your direct or lineal lines, but they can still be an important part of your family tree.

5. *Collateral relationships* are relationships between individuals who descend from common ancestors but are not related to each other in a direct line. These relationships include your brothers, sisters, aunts, uncles, nieces, nephews and cousins. You don't need to trace these collateral lines when researching your family tree, however, they can often lead you to clues about your ancestors if you come up against a brick wall. For example, you might find them as witnesses at a wedding, or Godparents at a baptism. I found two sisters who married the same man in the mid-1800s. The elder sister died in childbirth and her husband married the younger sister 2 months later, presumably to care for the 11 children he already had.

MORE EVIDENCE

Primary sources are created by someone who was an eye witness to an event. Secondary sources are created after the event by someone who was not there, or who may have recorded the event a long time later. They are hearsay or hindsight. They include textbooks, biographies, newspaper articles, movies, stories and musical recordings. A secondary source can be created from a wide variety of primary sources. A film maker or an author may use eyewitness accounts to write about an event or tell a story. A textbook may be written by a historian who has taken their account of events from many primary sources; eyewitness accounts, vital records, diaries. The important thing is to ensure that whatever the source you use, primary or secondary, it is;

- Suitable - refers directly to the question you are asking.

- Objective - is free from bias and opinion

- Current - is the latest edition or version

- Accurate - is factual and based on evidence

- Credible - the author or producer is an expert in that field

- Authoritative - can be trusted to be accurate and is verifiable

Here are some things you can do to be sure the sources you use are reliable.

- Read the introduction, go through the table of contents and the index, to determine if the source has sufficient and relevant information. Also, the information in the work should meet the required academic standard, for example you do not use a primary school textbook for a History BA.

- Prejudices and biased opinions will never be excluded from secondary sources. It is important to detect these. An introduction or preface will usually give an idea of the point of view of the writer. If it shows bias, use other secondary sources to get a balanced view.

- Look at the date of publication. It is important that secondary sources contain information that reflect the most recent discoveries in the field. Therefore, pay attention to, and use the newer edition.

- The reference list can tell you the type of sources used and how they can be verified. *If a secondary source does not have references do not use it.*

- Investigate the author. Is he or she an expert in the field and well-known? Is the publisher a reputable company that only publishes works of high academic quality?

ONLINE SEARCHING

With thousands of pages added to Google every day, 'googling it' does not give you the best source of information. Anyone with access to a computer and the Internet can put information on the Web. Therefore online resources must be carefully evaluated before being accepted. Ask;

- Is it produced by a reputable website? Look at website's address and see if it includes ".gov" or ".edu" Information from websites of government organizations and educational institutions tend to be more reliable.

- Does the webpage have an author? If the author's name is given, there must be verification that he or she has the expertise or qualifications in the subject.

- The webpage should give a list of sources used by the author. This would be helpful in verifying the information

Biographical
Database of Australia (BDA)

NSW State Records;

Indexes available online for immigrants to Sydney, Port Phillip, Moreton Bay and Newcastle

Immigration Agents' Lists & Immigration Board's Lists – look at both

Images of some passenger lists

Immigration deposit journals, 1853-65, 1875-1900

Reports by the Immigration Board on complaints of immigrants about their passage, 1838-87

Reports by the Immigration Agent on condition of immigrants and ships on their arrival, 1837-95

Victoria Public Records Office;

Unassisted overseas passengers 1852-1923

Assisted passengers 1839-1871

Assisted passengers after 1871 listed in Inwards Overseas Passenger Lists

http://www.prov.vic.gov.au/

South Australia;

Ships to SA 1836 to 1851

Lists ships by year – no global name search

Includes inter-colonial and overseas arrivals

www.slsa.sa.gov.au/fh/passengerlists/BoundforSouthAustralia.htm

Queensland,

QLD State Archives indexes to

Assisted Immigration 1848-1912

www.archives.qld.gov.au/research/indexes.asp

Also information in Ancestry.com

General Sites

Chapman Codes – https://www.gsq.org.au/index.php/services/research-guides/chapman-codes.html

What you can expect to see on an historical AUS BDM certificate - http://www.jaunay.com/bdm.html

 Explore the CoraWeb website for information on Australian birth death and marriage certificates. http://www.coraweb.com.au/categories/birth-death-and-marriage-records

SEARCH TIPS

SEARCHING CAN BE FRUSTRATING AND TIME CONSUMING.

Here are some hints and tips that might help you to conduct a more successful search.

- When you are searching online or in an index, it is tempting to put in as much information as possible. It is often better to put in less information.

- If you get too many results, you can add more information.

- Spelling used in early records can vary: names can be spelled in different ways or transcribed wrongly.

- Sometime people change their names.

- When trying to read difficult handwriting, compare the letter or combination of letters with a word you know. *Family Search* has an online aid to reading old handwriting.

- Never assume a family relationship with someone just because they have the same name.

- You will find that many records have similar information.

- If you are looking for a birth but can't find it in the official civil registration records, you may be able to find a baptism in church records or a newspaper birth notice.

- An address that is not in the electoral rolls might be in the post office directories. So, think creatively.

- Not all children were given a name by the time their birth was registered: in the 19th century Tasmanian civil registration indexes, for example, some unnamed children were registered as 'f' (for female) and 'm' (for male) instead of a given name. So, in the Tasmanian Names Index search for "SURNAME Given name not recorded"

- Family historians love to use abbreviations and acronyms. Start your own Abbreviation List and each time you come across an abbreviationthatisnewtoyou,addittoyourlist.

There are standard abbreviations for showing relationships in family records:

marriage	m or =
births	b
baptisms	bap or bp
deaths	d
burials	bur or bd
funerals	f

These will help you to understand records you find and other people's family trees. Using them will make your records clear to others.

BRICK WALLS

Every genealogist and family historian will run up against a brick wall at some stage in their research. Here are some strategies that may help to knock it down.

NAMES

Maiden names - Most countries have some kind of Social Security records. This is one of the few places on official records where maiden names may be found. Another extremely useful place to find a woman's maiden name are in court documents.

Divorce cases, property disputes, immigrant change of name, applications for guardianship of a child, etc all required a woman's maiden name.

It should be noted that in early court documents, a woman was often represented by her husband, father or uncle so be sure to search under their names as well.

Middle names - Names are more changeable than most people realise. People refer to themselves often on official records by their middle name. This can happen even once a person reaches middle age. Always cross check archival records by first name and middle name.

Common family names - Trying to trace the genealogy of a family with a common surname may come down to probabilities. For example, one way that you can shorten the odds in your favour is to look at the names of all the immediate family members.

Target your research at the person in the family with the least common first name. This will increase your chances of finding a successful match and also hopefully speed up the search process.

Short family names - People with short family names often mistakenly think there is little likelihood of a misspelling of their family name in old records. There is a possibility that the spelling of the family name has evolved over time.

For example, there is a distinct possibility that a family name that ends in a double letter, like the double 'l' in Tell may in the past have had an 'e' on the end of the name. Tell becomes Telle, Well becomes Welle, Bell becomes Belle. Always consider this possibility.

Aliases - In historical records, people used aliases all the times. A couple of common aliases: using the middle name as a last name, using the mother's maiden name as a last name and anglicising a non-English family name.

Surnames beginning with a vowel - Most genealogists are familiar with the need to check spelling variations of family names in old records. Become familiar with Soundex.

Soundex is a phonetic index that groups together names that sound alike but are spelled differently, for example, Stewart and Stuart.

Pay particular attention to family names that begin with a, e, i, o, u and y. These names are often misspelled in records by people adding a consonant in front of the vowel.

The most common consonant added to a family name in this kind of situation is an H. So a name like Abner becomes Habner, Illier becomes Hillier, etc. The reverse is also true for all names that begin with H. Consider searching the family name with the H removed.

Naming conventions - Many families and cultures have naming conventions, the way in which traditional family forenames are allocated to children according to the order in which they are born.

For example, it was common in Victorian England that the first male child was given the name of the father's father. The second male child was named after the mother's father. The third male child was named after the father. The first female child was named after the mother's mother and the second female child is named after the father's mother and the third female was named after the mother.

Knowledge of naming conventions can be used to determine the names of the parents and grandparents. You can make a reasonable guess as to the first names of the parents and grandparents if you know the names and order of birth of all the children. This naming convention had a downside. Children of the period often died at childbirth or at a very young age. It was not uncommon for the name of a parent or grandparent to be recycled or reused and given to the next child that was born. If you have an ancestor with a large family and two of the children have the same name, this tells you two things: the first child probably died before the second child was born, and the name has great significance to the family.

Some family historians feel uncomfortable recording the names of children who died at a young age. However, if your family does not remember them, then who will?

ADOPTION

When researching your ancestors, it is important to understand the difference between adopted and abandoned.

- ∞ Adoption is when someone who is not kin assumes the parenting of a child. It has been practiced throughout history, but it only became a common phenomenon in the 1920s or later.

- ∞ Adoption records can often be much more difficult to obtain and genealogists, and the adopted children themselves, are often at the mercy of legislative regulations. In some jurisdictions, adoption was a for-profit exercise. The people running the adoption business often had a vested interested in not keeping good records as to the origin of the children.

- ∞ Abandonment - Prior to the 1920s, most children without parents were abandoned.

- ∞ Abandoned children usually ended up in orphanages and/or placed out as indentured servants or apprentices for certain trades.

∞ Abandoned children are usually easier to trace because they were wards of the state or a non-profit organisation. To account for the funds needed to feed and maintain these children, ledgers were kept giving details of the children at orphanages and poorhouses.

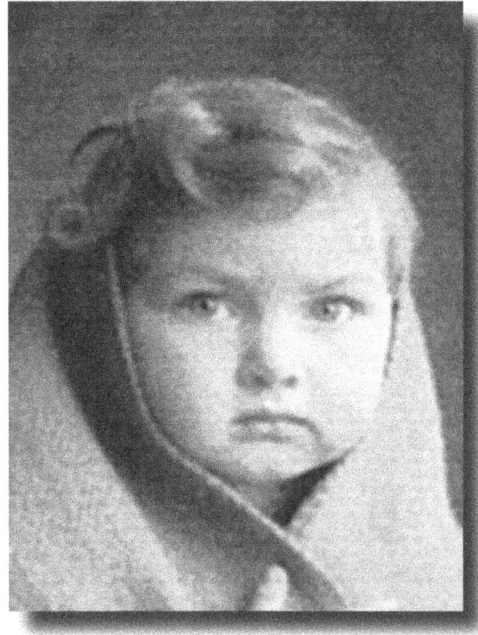

It is difficult to ascertain what percentage of children were historically adopted/abandoned (families rarely want to admit such issues), but adoptions in most countries today run from 1% to 3% and the numbers were almost certainly much higher one hundred years ago. Never discount adoption/abandonment as a possibility.

- ∞ Relatives raising children - A very common variant of adoption/abandonment is relatives raising a child. Sometimes you will come across a child in a family with a name used in another branch of the family. It is possible that the parents are raising a relative's child. Or sisters may have adopted children who are related to one another, typically the adopted children are brother and sister.

- ∞ Finally, when looking at old census records that list servants in a household, pay particular attention to the names of the servants. They could be distant relatives of the family.

IMMIGRATION

Return to country of birth - First generation migrants to a new region or country often got homesick for 'the old country'. When looking for an ancestor where the trail has run cold in the ancestor's later years, consider the possibility that they may have moved back to the region where they were born or where their parents were born. This is more common than most people realise.

Migrating family units - When a family migrates long distances, don't assume that all the children migrated with the parents. Check the age of the children at the time of migration. Older children may have stayed behind in the old country.

Land records - If your ancestors migrated to farm, they may have received a land grant. Always check federal and state government land grant records.

Place of birth - One of the great challenges of genealogy is dealing with conflicting information from different sources.

For example, a common problem is having two documents showing two different places of birth for the same individual.

Immigrants often change their name when they move to new countries, for example, immigrants moving to English-speaking countries often try to Anglicise their family name.

However, it does not necessarily end at just a name change. Over time immigrants will sometimes want to mask their place of birth and make it look like they were born in their new country, not their old country.

An immigrant may change their place of birth later in life if their real place of birth has fallen out of favour. For example, during World War I and II immigrants would hide the fact they were born in Germany or Italy.

Always consider this as a possibility when looking at conflicting information on place of birth and any other information that would tie an individual back to their birthplace. People often changed their place of birth after they had been in their new country for several years.

PLACE

Search by village - Family historians usually search for ancestors by name. However, if you can't find them by name and you know your ancestor came from a small town or village and you know the approximate date of the record you are looking for, consider performing a search by the village name for that date range. Small villages do not produce that many records and a search may produce surprises, like previously unknown relatives.

Street names changes - Over time, some villages grow into towns. However, towns rarely grow into cities. What usually happens is that several towns close to each other merge to form a city. When this happens there are often too many streets with the same name. For example, every town has a *Church St* but a city can only have one *Church St*. Some streets in the former towns had to change names. The Church St that is on your ancestor's record may not be the same Church St today. Consult an old map of the region before the formation of the city.

Local histories - Local histories can be an invaluable source of clues as to what happened to family members. They typically contain major events in the region that could have impacted the lives of your ancestors. A major drought or a major flood, military conflicts, disease or social influences can play a major role in migrations. If there a mass exodus of people leaving the region, the local history will give some clue as to where they went.

Changing boundaries - State, municipal, county and country lines change over time. When searching for old state and county records, make sure you have the correct county for the time period in question.

Towns and occupations - During the industrial revolution, right through to the present, certain towns were associated with certain industries. For example, Elizabeth in South Australia was a centre for automobile manufacture. If you think your ancestor may have moved, consider researching the history of the town. It can give a clue as to the occupation of your ancestor.

LOCAL OR REGIONAL RECORDS

Local schools and their records - If your ancestor comes from a small town or village, you may want to consider writing to the local school. As well, don't forget the children in the local school are the living descendants of the people from the region. It is quite possible that one of the parents of the children would know something about the person or family you are researching. School records are a resource often overlooked. Schools always kept detailed class rolls. Schools also took class pictures, which is an excellent way to find photographs of your ancestors when they were children. School records can also be used to confirm dates for an ancestor. Children often went to school for several years. It is only necessary to find your ancestor listed in just one school year to be able to make a reasonable estimate of their year of birth. Therefore, always try to determine where your ancestor may have gone to school and then see if the school records are still available. Typically, old school records are located at the local archives or held by the State Education Department.

Poorhouses - Poorhouses go by various names in various countries and over different periods of time. However, they always share one common trait of providing welfare and living assistance to those in need. Since this assistance comes at a financial cost, local authorities always recorded and documented who received the aid. Thus, the poorest people in society often had the best records kept on them. Search the Poorhouse and Workhouse records to see if any of your ancestors are there.

Electoral rolls - Electoral rolls are kept to allow local authorities to know who is registered to vote. They are often updated on schedule with a much higher frequency than census records. Looking through electoral rolls is a good way to narrow down the date range to find out when somebody died or moved out of a region. Electoral rolls are arguably the most powerful yet overlooked resource available to genealogists. Countries that do not have census records usually kept electoral rolls.

Directories - City directories sorted by street address can also be a valuable source of information. City or street directories often listed useful information such as the occupation of the resident. As well, immigrants to a place often wanted to live near relatives. Researching who lived within two blocks of your ancestor can often produce several previously unknown aunts, uncles and cousins.

CHURCHES

Neighbourhood church/place of worship - Most local religious organisations kept records of their active members. Often, these list the full name of each individual, sometimes the date of birth, and place of origin. Besides providing such information, these records also provide an excellent date range for determining when someone moved or died.

Vanished church/place of worship - During times when government records were sparse or nonexistent, records from religious organisations often provide the best ancestral information. Churches are an excellent place to find records of births, marriages and burials.

Do not be discouraged if the church of your ancestor has been torn down or disbanded over the years. This does not mean the records have disappeared. Often the records were passed to regional government offices. Always check out this possibility.

DEATH

Mortality tables - When estimating the age of death of an ancestor try to find a mortality table for the country of your ancestors. A mortality table is a statistical table that shows how long people of each age are expected to live and how frequent deaths are for a given age or occupation. The Internet contains historic mortality tables for several countries. If you cannot find one, consider contacting the main government statistical agency for your country. Alternatively, consider contacting a life insurance company. Life insurance companies use mortality tables to calculate policy premiums. Use historic mortality tables, not current mortality tables. People live much longer these days.

Mortuary records - Mortuary records at funeral homes often list the full names and place of origin of next of kin. Typically, this will mean that mortuary records often have the full names and origin of the parents of the deceased. This is an excellent way to find out names and places of the previous generation. It always pays to look at the mortuary records in a funeral home.

Funeral sign-in books - Funeral sign-in books are those books that all visitors are asked to sign when they go to a funeral. They are usually given to the family at the end of the funeral. If you can gain access to a funeral sign-in book, it can provide a wealth of information about your ancestors. Funerals are typically attended by family members both close and distant on the family tree. This is a great way to get leads on missing branches of the family.

Walk the cemetery - A simple, but effective, genealogy brick-wall solution for ancestors that came from small towns is to take a walk through the local cemetery. This is a good way to look for clues by reading the inscriptions on the tombstones. Many cemeteries are divided by religion. You can save yourself much time and narrow your search in the cemetery if you happen to know the religion of your ancestors.

Neighbours in the cemetery - Families often buy several plots in a cemetery. Usually these plots are located next to each other. When you are visiting the grave-site of an ancestor always take photographs of the neighbouring grave-sites. They could be your relatives. Sometimes this is not obvious at the time but it can become more apparent at a later date. For example, two sisters could buy neighbouring family plots. The sisters have both married and have different last names. They may not look like they are related when you glance at the tombstones. Always be safe and take some photographs of neighbouring tombstones. With digital cameras this is a quick and simple thing to do. Alternatively, check online at the many websites that now show tombstone pictures.

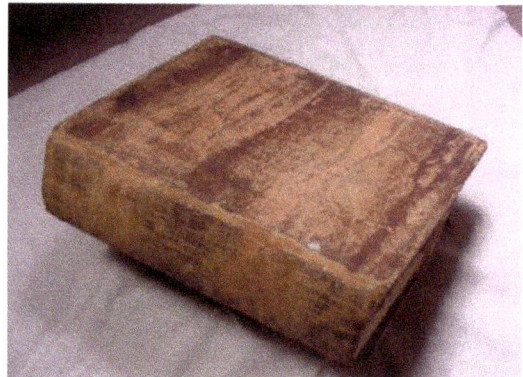

FAMILY BIBLES

One hundred years ago most people were either illiterate or barely literate. The typical household had only a handful of books. One of these books was almost certainly a family bible (or other religious text)and was the only book they would ever read. It was also where many people would write down important information the names and birthdays of family members. Ask your relatives if they have an old family bible. Check the blank pages on the inside front and back covers and you may make an incredible family discovery.

FAMILY

Existing family trees - In most families, there is usually one person (often a distant relative) who has spent the time and energy to put together the family tree. It is always a good idea to ask around the family to see if a family tree has already been created.

Most genealogists know this and they also know to look at online family trees from various resources (try our Family Tree Search Engine which checks online family trees and genealogy forums).

One often overlooked resource for family trees are the local libraries near where your ancestors lived. Especially in small towns, a collection of published family histories in local libraries will often touch on some part of your family tree.

Picture in a frame - There is one simple exercise that should always be done with old family pictures that are framed. Take the photograph out of the frame and examine the back of the image. People often write notes on the back as to where the picture was taken and who is in the photograph.

This same trick can be used on family jewellery. Always inspect family jewellery (especially rings and bracelets) closely with a magnifying glass. Check for engravings of names and dates on the inside. Also check for stamps and other marks of the jeweller. This can be used to date the age of the jewellery.

Shotgun weddings - A shotgun wedding is a wedding where the bride is already pregnant. Families rarely like to talk about shotgun weddings, but the reality is that shotgun weddings are common. When trying to estimate the date of birth of a child from a wedding date (or vice versa) do not assume there is a minimum nine-month gap between the two dates. It could be much shorter. The child could even have been born before the wedding date. This type of situation is more common than most people.

Skip a generation - Most people build their family tree by starting with themselves and working backward. This doesn't work well when you come across an ancestor who cannot be found simply because they never wanted to be found. People trying to escape debts, trying to escape businesses that have failed and trying to escape questionable behaviour all had an incentive not to be found. Even people who were never married or were married but never had children can often be difficult to trace. The solution - skip a generation.

Try researching their parents first. Often a detailed knowledge of an ancestor's parents can shed light on what happened to their children. You might even find your missing ancestor turning up in unexpected places, like a funeral sign-in book when one of the parents died.

Widows remarrying - Except for the last couple of decades, economic necessity usually required a widow with children to remarry fairly quickly. It was not uncommon for a woman would remarry within three to four months of the death of her late husband. As well, women usually picked the church where they were married. These two facts can be used to your advantage.

One way to trace the marriage of a widow is to start with the local church records from the date of the wake of her late husband and read forward on a day-by-day basis. Don't be surprised to find a wedding within six months.

This trick also works backwards. Start on the wedding day of the widow and go backward in time a couple of months and you will probably find the details on the death of the previous husband.

Elderly parents - Elderly or widowed parents often went to live with one of their children. Always consider this possibility when you lose track of someone later in their life.

Wills - Wills are a golden source of information for genealogists. Wills are always written by the deceased and they are legally binding documents. Therefore, wills contain accurate spelling of names, correct dates, correct addresses and a correct list of the property owned by the deceased.

They also list all of a person's aliases and variants and a list of all immediate family members, such as siblings. Ask family members if they have any old wills of your ancestors or spend the time tracking down the will at the local probate court.

OTHER

Search sideways - When you get stuck and have trouble tracing the parents of your ancestors, consider taking a different path. You may have inadvertently stumbled upon an ancestor who was the black sheep of the family and did not have much interaction with the parents.

Take a closer look at the brothers and sisters of your ancestor instead. This may ultimately lead you to the parents.

Contact distant living relatives through the grave - If you track down an ancestor to a particular grave-site in an old graveyard, look at how well the grave-site is maintained relative to the neighbouring grave-sites.

If the grave-site is better maintained than other grave-sites in the cemetery it is a good indication that someone with a connection to your ancestor lives in the area. Consider leaving a message at the grave-site with all your contact details. However, this is not email, so don't expect a reply within a week. It will likely take months, or never, before someone replies. Make sure you leave the message in a well-sealed container and firmly attach it to the grave-site. Also, if necessary, inform the cemetery staff to make sure they are okay with the procedure and to make sure they do not throw your message out. They may even know who is maintaining the grave-site.

Retirement homes - Retirement homes (especially those run by non-profit organisations) would often take on senior citizens with no money. In order to cover their costs, they would often attempt to track down family members. Part of this process involved interviewing the senior citizen to try to establish family connections. These records may have been kept by the retirement home. These records can be an effective way to find other ancestors.

Family timelines - One obvious brick wall solution is to check key family dates across generations to look for inconsistencies. For example, children cannot be born after their mother has died or more than nine months after their father has died. Children cannot be born if the mother is too young or too old.

A simple rechecking of dates can help eliminate erroneous data and can also be used to narrow down estimated date ranges. For large, complicated families, consider building a family timeline in a spreadsheet to check for consistency across dates.

Family recipe books - Family recipe books are almost as common as family trees. Oddly enough, there can be a connection between the two of them that can be exploited by an astute genealogist.

For example, one of the biggest hurdles that genealogists can face is when an ancestor has migrated to a new country and anglicised their name. Trying to find out where they came from can often become an involved exercise.

Here is a novel approach. Look through the family recipe book. For example, a number of Polish recipes would suggest that your ancestors came from Poland. Even within a country, certain dishes can be very local in origination.

Do a bit of research on unusual dishes or dishes that use unusual ingredients and you may be able to narrow down your search to a particular area of a country. Sometimes it pays to think with your stomach!

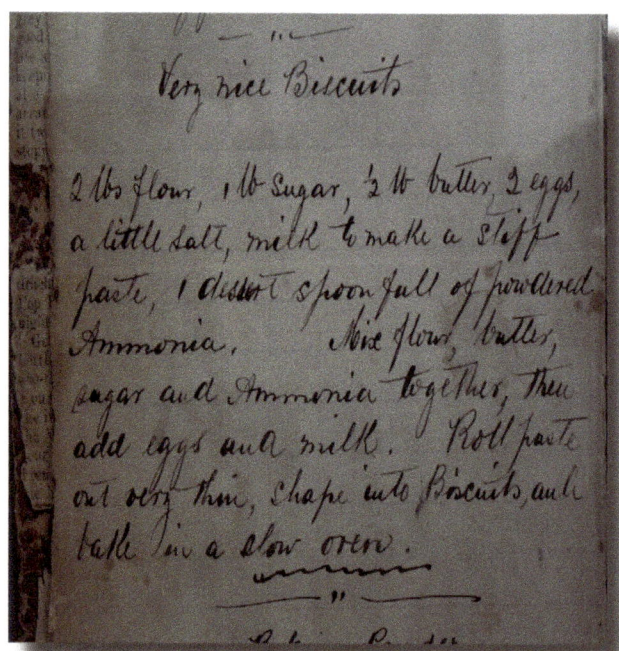

GLOSSARY

There are lots of unfamiliar words in the language of Genealogy and Family History. Here's a glossary to help you decipher the language in some of the records or references you may use.

  ❧ **ahnentafel** [ahnen: ""ancestors""" + tafel: ""table""]. Tabulates the ancestry of one individual by generation in text rather than pedigree chart format. A comprehensive ahnentafel gives more than the individual's name, date and place of birth, christening, marriage, death and burial. It should give biographical and historical commentary for each person listed, as well as footnotes citing the source documents used to prove what is stated.

  ❧ **ahnentafel number** unique number assigned to each position in an ancestor table. Number one designates the person in the first generation, the one at the beginning of the chart. Numbers two and three designate the parents of number one; the second generation. Numbers four to seven designate the grandparents of person number one; the third generation. As the ahnentafel extends by generation, the number of persons doubles.

  ❧ **Ancestor** A person from whom you descend; grandparents, great-grandparents, 2nd great-grandparents (also called great great-grandparents), 3rd great-grandparents, etc.; direct-line ancestor; forefather; forebear

  ❧ **Ancestry** Denotes all of your ancestors from your parents as far back as they are traceable. Estimates suggest that everyone has approximately 65,000 traceable ancestors, meaning ancestors whose existence can be documented in surviving records.

  ❧ **annotation** Interpretation, explanation, clarification, definition, or supplement. Genealogical presentations contain statements, record sources, documents, conclusions, or other historical information that require an annotation.

  ❧ **Authenticate** The process to prove a document is not a forgery

  ❧ **banns** Public announcement of an intended marriage, generally made in church

  ❧ **base-born** Illegitimate child

  ❧ **bastard** Illegitimate child

  ❧ **bequeath** To leave or give property to another person or organization (used in wills)

  ❧ **bibliography** List of writings relating to a specific subject, some of which are annotated. A bibliographic citation describes and identifies the author, edition, date of issue, publisher, and typography of a book or other written material.

  ❧ **birth record** A birth record contains information about the birth of an individual. On a birth record, you can usually find the mother's full maiden name and the father's full name, the name of the baby, the date of the birth, and county where the birth took place. Many birth records include other information, such as the birthplaces of the baby's parents, the addresses of the parents, the number of children that the parents have, the race of the parents, and the parents' occupations.

  ❧ **cemetery records** Records of the names and death dates of those buried in a cemetery or graveyard.

  ❧ **census records** An official enumeration of the population in a particular area. In addition to counting the inhabitants of an area, the census generally collects other vital information, such as names, ages, citizenship status, and ethnic background..

  ❧ **christian name** Names other than a person's last name

  ❧ **church records** Formal documents that churches have kept about their congregations through the years; christenings, baptisms, marriages, and burials.

  ❧ **collateral line** Line of descent connecting persons who share a common ancestor, but are related through an aunt, uncle, cousin, nephew, etc.

ও **consanguinity** Degree of relationship between persons who descend from a common ancestor. A father and son are related by lineal consanguinity, uncle and nephew by collateral sanguinity.

ও **common ancestor** Person through whom two or more persons claim descent or lineage

ও **consort** Wife, husband, spouse, mate, or companion

ও **cousin** Child of an aunt or uncle; in earlier times, this could be a kinsman, close relative, or friend

ও **daughter-in-law** The wife of an individual's son; also used to mean a step-daughter (see step-)

ও **deceased** Someone who has died; commonly written ""the deceased""

ও **descendant** Anyone to whom an individual is an ancestor—their children, grandchildren, great-grandchildren, and so on

ও **direct line** Line of decent traced through persons who are directly related to one another as a child and parent

ও **directories** A variety of records containing an alphabetical/classified listing of names, addresses, and such as information for city, telephone, county, regional, professional, post office, street, ethnic, and school environments.

ও **Dissenter** Label given a person who refused to belong to the established Church of England

ও **double date** More than one date given for an event. The practice of writing double dates resulted from switching from the Julian to the Gregorian calendar. This also relates to the fact that not all countries and people accepted the new calendar at the same time.

ও **dowager** Widow holding property or a title received from her deceased husband; title given in England to widows of princes, dukes, earls, and other noblemen

ও **dower** Legal provision of real estate and support made to the widow for her lifetime from a husband's estate

ও **dowry** Land, money, goods, or personal property brought by a bride to her husband in marriage; also spelled dowery

ও **Emigrant** Person leaving one country to reside in another country

ও **Emigration** Departing the home country to live in another country

ও **estate** Assets and liabilities of a decedent, including land, personal belongings and debts

ও **evidence** Any kind of proof, such as testimony, documents, records, certificates, material objects, etc.

ও **family group sheet** A form that presents genealogical information about a nuclear family

ও **family pedigrees** In general, family pedigrees refer to family group sheets that are linked as a continuing lineage.

ও **family histories** Books that detail the basic genealogical facts about one or more generations of a particular family

ও **Freeman** Male of legal age with the right to vote, own land and practice a trade

ও **full age** Age of majority; legal age; adult (legal age varied according to place and current law)

ও **Gazetteer** A book that alphabetically names and describes places in a specific area. For example, a county gazetteer would name and describe the towns, lakes, rivers, and mountains in the county.

ও **GEDCOM** (acronym) GEnealogy Data COMmunications A standardised format for genealogy databases that allows the exchange of data among different software programs and operating systems.

ও **Genealogy** Study of one's ancestry; summary history or table of a person's ancestry

ও **good brother** Brother-in-law

ও **good sister** Sister-in-law

ও **good son** Son-in-law

ও **grand-dame** Grandmother

ও **guardian** Person lawfully appointed to care for the person of a minor, invalid, incompetent and his or her interests, such as education, property management and investments

- **Heir** Person who succeeds, by the rules of law, to an estate upon the death of an ancestor; one with rights to inherit an estate

- **heir apparent** By law a person whose right of inheritance is established, provided he or she outlives the ancestor. see

- **Illegitimate Child** born to a woman who is not married to the father

- **Immigrant Person** moving into a country from another country

- **Immigration** The process of moving into a new country to live

- **in lloco parentis** In the stead of one or both parents

- **indentured servant** Person who is bound into the service of another person for a specified period, usually seven years in the 18th and 19th centuries, to repay the passage to the new country

- **index** An alphabetical list of names that were taken from a particular set of records. For example, a census record index lists the names of individuals that are found in a particular set of census records. You can also find them on CD-ROM, microfilm, microfiche and the Internet.

- **infant** Person under legal age

- **instant** of this month

- **IGI** (acronym) **International Genealogical Index**, a resource of the Family History Library of the Church of Jesus Christ of Latter-day Saints. Containing more than 300 million names, it is an index of the people submitted as part of family trees, or extracted from microfilmed church or public records from as far back as the 1500s.

- **Intestate** Used to denote a person who died without leaving a will

- **Inventory** A legal list of all the property in a deceased person's estate. The executor of the will is required to make an inventory.

- **Issue Children**, descendants, offspring

- **Joiner** Carpenter who does finish work

- **Julian Calendar** Calendar named for Julius Caesar and used from 45 B.C. to A.D. 1582, called the ""Old Style"" calendar; replaced by the Gregorian calendar

- **Knave** Servant boy

- **land records** Deeds; proof that a piece of land has been legally transferred to a particular individual. The information you receive from the records will vary, but you will at least get a name, the location of the property, and the period of ownership.

- **Lineage** Direct line of descent from an ancestor; progeny

- **local history** Usually, a book about a particular town or county. Local histories were quite popular in the late 19th century. They usually also include some information about the important families who lived there

- **maiden name** A woman's surname prior to marriage

- **major** Person who has reached legal age

- **majority** Legal age (varies according to country)

- **Manuscripts** Usually, unpublished family histories or collections of family papers. Depending on what the manuscript contains, you may be able to find all kinds of family information.

- **marriage bond** Document obtained by an engaged couple prior to marriage. It affirmed that there was no moral or legal reason why the couple could not be married. In addition, the man affirmed that he would be able to support himself and his new bride.

- **marriage contract** Legal agreement between prospective spouses made before marriage to determine their property rights and those of their children

- **marriage records** Record containing information about a marriage between two individuals. On a marriage record, you can at least find the bride's and groom's full names, the date of the marriage, and county where the marriage took place. Many marriage records include other information, such as the names and birthplaces of the bride's and groom's parents, the addresses of the bride and groom, information about previous marriages, and the names of the witnesses to the marriage.

- **maternal line** Line of descent traced through the mother's ancestry

- **matron** Older married woman with children

- **military records** An account of those working for the armed forces.
- **Minor** A person under legal age; historically, the legal age differed from place to place and over time (Check prevailing law to determine the legal age requirement at a specific time.)
- **naturalization records** Documents recording the process by which an immigrant becomes a citizen.
- **Nee** Born, used to denote a woman's maiden name (e.g., Anne Gibson nee West)
- **newspaper announcements** Recorded events within newspapers of genealogical interest, such as births, deaths, and marriages.
- **oral history** A collection of family stories told by a member of the family or by a close family friend.
- **orphan asylum** An institution for the care and protection of children without parents; orphanage
- **paleography** Study of handwriting
- **parish** Ecclesiastical division or jurisdiction; the site of a church
- **passenger lists** Compilation of the names and information about passengers who arrived on ships
- **paternal line** Line of descent traced through the father's ancestry
- **patronymics** the practice of creating last names from the name of one's father; for example, Robert, John's son, would become Robert Johnson.

- **Pedigree** A person's ancestry, lineage, family tree
- **pedigree chart** A chart showing a person's ancestry
- **pension** A benefit paid regularly to a person after retirement from work or military service or suffering a work/military service- related disability, or to a surviving spouse or surviving children after the death of the pensioner.

- **pensioner** Person who receives any kind of pension benefits
- **poll** Used in early tax records denoting a taxable person; person eligible to vote
- **posthumous** A child born after the death of the father; any action after an individual's death
- **primary source** Records created at the time of an event. A primary source for a birth date would be a birth certificate. While birth dates are on other documents, such as marriage certificates, they are not be primary sources because they were not created at the time of the birth.
- **Primogeniture** Insures the right of the eldest son to inherit the entire estate of his parents, to the exclusion of younger sons.
- **probate records** Documents recording the disposition of a deceased individual's property.
- **Progeniture** A direct ancestor
- **public domain** Land owned by a government
- **Reeve** Churchwarden; early name for sheriff in England
- **relliicta** Widow
- **relliictus c** Widower
- **relict** Widow;
- **secondary evidence** Evidence that is inferior to primary evidence or the best evidence
- **secondary source** A record that was created a significant amount of time after an event occurred.
- **sibling** A brother or sister, persons who share the same parents
- **siic** Term signifying that a copy reads exactly as the original; indicates a possible mistake in the original.
- **Soundex** (acronym) Sound Index Phonetic indexing system
- **Source** The document, record, publication, manuscript, etc. used to prove a fact
- **Sponsor** An individual, other than the parents of a child, who takes responsibility for the child's religious education. Sponsors are usually present at a child's baptism. Sponsors are often referred to as godparents.
- **step-** Used in conjunction with a degree of kinship by marriage
- **stepchild** Child of one of the spouses by a former marriage who has not been adopted by the step-parent

- **stepfather** Husband of a child's mother by a later marriage
- **stepmother** Wife of a child's father by a later marriage
- **surname** Last name, family name
- **Titheable** A person taxable by law
- **Tithe** English law: the tenth part of one's annual increase paid to support noblemen and clergy; amount of annual poll tax
- **Transcribe** To make a full, written (or typewritten) copy of a record, book, or other document or written work
- **Transcript** Something transcribed, especially a written, typewritten or printed copy. In a transcript, it is assumed that everything from the original was transcribed or copied.
- **Valid** That which is legal and binding
- **Vestry** Administrative group within a parish; the ruling body of a church
- **vital records** Birth, marriage, death and divorce records
- **wheelwright** Person who makes and repairs vehicle wheels, such as carts, wagons, etc.
- **witness** A witness is an individual present at an event such as a marriage or the signing of a document who can vouch that the event took place

ADD ANY OTHER TERMINOLOGY YOU FIND HERE;

USEFUL REPOSITORIES

Barry J Ewell, Family Treasures: 15 Lessons, Tips, and Tricks for Discovering Your Family (Cedar Fort Publishing, 2012) Free extracts from this text are available online.

Tips and Methods to Build Your Family Tree - https://clanmacnicol.org/conducting-research

Recommendations by Clifford L. Wolf on conducting research (Clan MacNicol Federation).

Reading Handwriting

If you need help with interpreting handwriting, see the following Family Search resources:

- Handwriting Helps - https://familysearch.org/indexing/help/handwriting
- FamilySearch Category: Handwriting - https://familysearch.org/learn/wiki/en Category:Handwriting

Repositories

- CoraWeb (Cora Num's website)
- National Library of Australia eResources - Offers home access to over 100 subscription databases.
- Trove - For Australian newspapers online, see Trove Digitised Newspapers and More
- National Archives of Australia - The NAA holds Commonwealth (Australian) government records from 1901. Online services include RecordSearch and PhotoSearch.
- Tasmanian Archive and Heritage Office This archive has state and non-state records, such as parish registers.
- Australian Joint Copying Project Guide - A guide to a collection of historical material relating to Australia, New Zealand and the Pacific from 1560 to 1984.
- Findmypast.com.au - One of many genealogy websites designed for searching records. Compare this with Ancestry's Library Edition.
- Family Search Free access to the library of the Church of Jesus Christ of Latter Day Saints.
- Family History and Historical Societies in Australia This is another comprehensive Cora Num list.
- Federation of Family History Societies (United Kingdom)

Civil Registration

- FreeBMD (United Kingdom)

Dating Photographs

- Family photos: what are they wearing?
- Jayne Shrimpton's website

WIDENING THE SEARCH

INTRODUCTION

- ↝ Has your family tree grown?

- ↝ Have you started to add more generations of great grandparents? Or added some brothers and sisters, aunts, uncles and cousins?

- ↝ Is there someone that has you intrigued? There is a mystery surrounding their life, or an old family myth that you would like to prove or disprove.

If you have answered 'Yes' to any or all of these questions, you probably need to go further that the vital records. You need to use other sources of information. There are many places in which your ancestor may have left a trail for you to follow;

- ↝ convict records

- ↝ immigration records

- ↝ military records

- ↝ newspapers

- ↝ history books

- ↝ diaries

- ↝ letters

- ↝ journals

- ↝ stock and station records

ASKING THE RIGHT QUESTIONS

Online records are housed in databases. Databases contain many thousands, sometimes millions of records. Each records is divided into fields; that is, containers for each kind of information. The database selects records by matching the words you put into each field with a record that has the same words in those fields.

To be successful, you need to ask the database the right question. For example, if you enter Smith into the *last name* field on the search screen and John into the *first name* field on the search screen and press Return, the database will go and find every record that matches for every year it covers.

If that is Family Search or Ancestry.com there are going to be records retrieved from at least the 16th Century to the present. So you see, just a name is not enough.

Retrieving only the information you need from all of those records is the aim of the game.

You need to refine your search by being as specific as you can.

Start with formulating a good question.

For example. What regiment did Robert Andrew Mayor serve in during World War I?

Now choose which database you will use. It is no good looking in the NSW Registrar's database of Births, Marriages and Deaths to find a soldier's military record. You need to go to a military records database.

Once you know where to look, make a list of search words from information you already have;

- ↝ first name/s,

- ↝ last name,

- ↝ date of birth, and

- ↝ anything that is unique to that person and will reduce the number of records retrieved.

In the case of searching for a military record, these could be the defence force (army, navy or air-force) he/she served in, their service number or the date/year of enlistment. They are unique and will cut down on the number of results.

No matter what online records you need to search, the principles are the same;

- ✌ Plan your search carefully.

- ✌ Choose the right database.

- ✌ You do not have to complete all fields, but search by at least a last name, birth date, and state or county.

- ✌ Completing many search fields will yield fewer results, while completing fewer search fields usually returns more search results.

- ✌ Search with the information that is most likely to be on the records you are searching.

- ✌ If you don't have exact information, you can estimate it.

- ✌ When searching for a woman, search with her <u>maiden name</u> to find records created before marriage. Use her married name to find records created after marriage. You can also search with just her first name and the name/s of her spouse or parents.

- ✌ If you don't get the results you want, try adding or removing information. For example, if you searched with a birth city and county, you can try just searching with the county.

The old adage, "If at first you don't you don't succeed, try, try again", applies to online searching. If your search returns no results;

- ✌ Look at your key words and see if they could be spelled differently. For example, "Edmund" could be Edmond" or "Ned". Wild cards can be used for searching. Depending on the database the wild card may be * or % . Check the help screens to find out. Wild cards replace letters that could be different. So to find "Edmund" you would use a wild card in place of u to make sure that if the name has been spelled with an o, it can be found. "Edm*nd" or if you want to make sure it wasn't recorded as Edward by mistake, you can use a wildcard to replace all of the letters at the end - Ed*. Wild cards are very useful.

- ✌ Try taking out some of the keywords, like spouse, or parents. It may be that there is a record prior to marriage, or a different parent name.

Don't give up. Eventually you will knock down that brick wall. With practice you will get very good at searching.

Let's dive into some of the database records that you will use to track your ancestors, in and out of Australia.

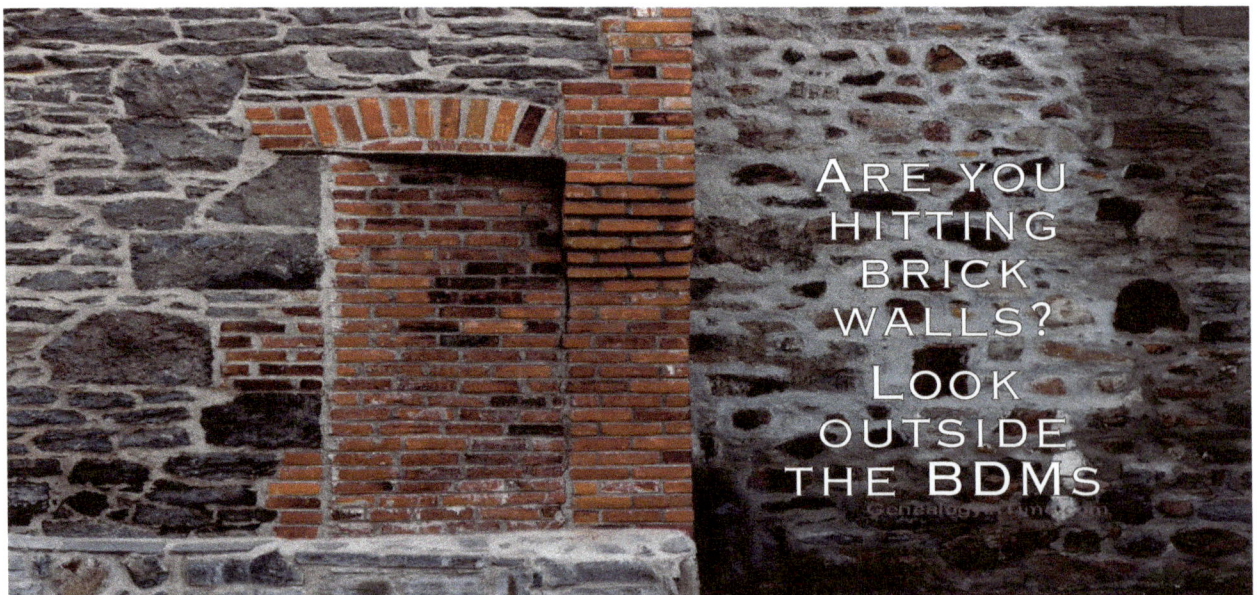

ARE YOU HITTING BRICK WALLS? LOOK OUTSIDE THE BDMs

Convicts, Immigrants and ANZACs

Convicts & Outcasts

TRANSPORTATION, PUNISHMENT OR SLAVERY?

Between 1788 and 1868, about 162,000 convicts were transported by the British government to the colonies of NSW, Van Diemen's Land and West Australia. How did they came to be transported across 12,000 miles of ocean, in chains, to a place where they had to build the infrastructure and grow the food for a new colony, in an unknown environment with unfamiliar seasons and unknown species of plants and animals? For those on the First Fleet, convict and jailer alike, it must have been a terrifying ordeal.

To understand their criminality, we need to go back to the social conditions of the time. Economically, the Industrial Revolution and a subsequent economic depression had left many living in poverty. It was also a time of political unrest. To when to rise up in protest against government, the established Church or social conditions brought swift reprisal and imprisonment.

In the past, we were taught that the convicts sent to Australia were a miserable lot, the criminal element of a country whose jails were overflowing with thieves, pickpockets and the dregs of humanity; that Britain needed somewhere to get rid of its outcasts and to create more prison accommodation. Transportation was the solution for British authorities, to send their criminals as far away as possible and leave them there. We now know that many transported convicts were far from the illiterate and impoverished outcasts that we have been led to expect. Many indeed were highly intelligent and well educated and went on to make valuable contributions to the growth and development of the young settlement. A walk through the Court Records of the Old Bailey between 1740 and 1860 tells this story well. Explore the *The Proceedings of the Old Bailey, 1674-1913* website at https://www.oldbaileyonline.org/index.jsp. Searching the sentence of Transportation will retrieve 41,239 cases of transportation, not all of whom were thugs, thieves and pickpockets.

An examination of the world in the 18th, 19th and early 20th centuries gives us a different understanding of transportation than the one we might already have. The 17th, 18th and 19th centuries were a time of colonisation of large parts of the rest of the world by European Governments and trading companies such as the Dutch East India Company. Colonisation resulted in;

- ☙ unprecedented movement of people from one continent or country to the other and
- ☙ a biological exchange of plants and animals from one part of the globe to another.

Colonisation depended upon cheap labour. During the early years of colonisation, European settlements in North America, the Caribbean and Australia had difficulties finding enough labour to build the necessary infrastructure and provide food and shelter for their people. The European settlements were either too thinly populated, impacted upon by disease, or occupied by populations unwilling to engage with the settlers. Their labour force, therefore, had to come from three main sources:

- ☙ Slaves
- ☙ Indentured servants/assisted migrants
- ☙ Convicts

In the North American colonies, all three forms of labour were used.

In Australia, there were not large scale systems of slavery, but there were significant flows of both convicts and Indentured servants. Convicts transported to Australia made up less than half of those transported in the British Empire.

If you wish to explore the history of penal transportation further, go to this site from the University of Leicester in the UK.

http://convictvoyages.org/map

Convict transportation was very similar to slavery and indenture. Your convict ancestors were more than criminals, they were also captive workers whose labour was needed to build the new colony. These factors change how we need to think about the records that describe their lives.

Convict labour arose out of the indenture system. Under the indenture system, migrants could reimburse the costs of their transport to the colonies by agreeing to work for a master for a period of some years for no wages other than the cost of clothing, housing and food.

The average length of an indenture signed by servants was four years. The minimum sentence to transportation for a convict was 7 years. This term was fixed in the 17th century to ensure that convict labour would be acceptable to settlers in England's colonies.

Convict minimum sentences were 7 years, up to 14 years or life, making convict labour attractive to settlers. They could take on a convict as a servant or labourer in the knowledge that the person was bound to work for them for a longer period of time than an indentured migrant.

The sentence that was imposed upon convicted offenders was fixed, not for legal reasons, but economic.

When convicts were transported to Australia from 1787 on, the minimum sentence to transportation was kept. This was to ensure that the cheap labour they performed was sufficient to cover the costs of getting them to Australia.

British transportation picked up after the passing of the transportation Act in 1718, but slowed after the American Revolution. There are peaks during the 1st, 2nd and 3rd fleets, and then a huge rise in the number of transported convicts sent overseas after the Napoleonic Wars.

Most of these convicts were sent to Australia, but around 13,000 were sent to Bermuda and Gibraltar. Then, from the late 1830s onwards, the numbers started to go down, declining rapidly after transportation to NSW ceased in 1840, Tasmania in 1853 and finally WA in 1868. Of the convicts sent out of Europe in the period 1415 to 1954, those shipped to Australia were a small proportion.

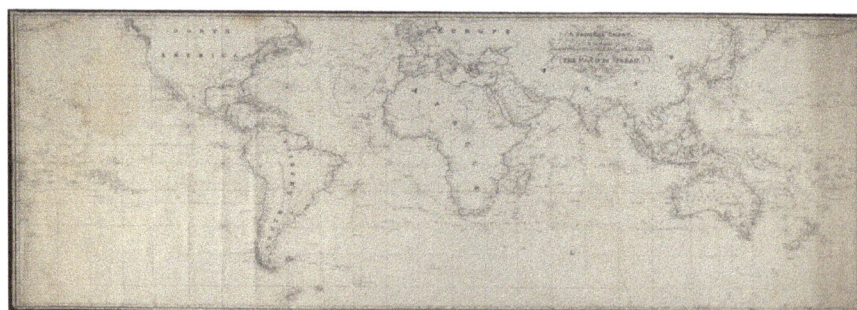

THE BRITISH JUSTICE SYSTEM IN THE 18TH & 19TH CENTURIES

In order to understand the records of trial and punishment of our convict ancestors in the 18th and 19th centuries it's important to know how the justice system worked in Britain in that period. It was very different to today.

In the 18th century justice was essentially a private system. A police service and prosecutors paid for by the government from the public purse was non existent. Under English law, any Englishman could prosecute any crime. Constables were appointed in some villages, their wages paid for by the local parish. There was no system of training or education in the law or individual's rights. Wages were low and subsidised by the payment he received from victims for arresting those accused of crime.

The prosecutor was usually the victim of the crime. It was up to the victim to file charges with the local magistrate, present evidence to the grand jury, and, if the grand jury found a case could be made, provide evidence and witnesses for the trial.

The arrest was made by the victim. Often the victim hired a watchman or a constable to make the arrest for him.

CONSTABLES

The local Parish Constable acted as a custodian until the accused could be brought before a magistrate.

Constables were chosen from among the householders of the parish, and served, unpaid, for a year, alongside their regular employment. Many constables paid substitutes to serve in their place. Most of their constabulary time was taken up with reacting to information given to them in the form of reports of crimes, or warrants issued by justices of the peace.

They were obliged to execute all warrants for arrest and orders given through the courts, justices of the peace, sheriffs and coroners for their jurisdiction. In addition, they were expected to respond to allegations and reports of felonies committed, and arrest those who they witnessed committing felonies and misdemeanours. Most of their efforts were reactive. By the Victorian period, the local or parish Constables were proving

ineffective in many areas. As crime rates rose, the Office of Constable had deteriorated to such an extent that they were often depicted as figures of fun, or irresponsible drunkards, little better than those they were arresting. Even when they took their responsibilities seriously, their powers were strictly limited by their immediate superiors, the magistrates.

THE WATCH

The parishes also employed evening patrols in the late eighteenth and early nineteenth centuries. The watch generally operated from 9pm or 10pm until 5am, 6am or 7am and evening patrols were generally employed to patrol from dusk until the setting of the watch in the evening, and also sometimes in the morning. The watchmen and patrols were often monitored by the parish or ward constable and beadle. Some characteristics of the modern police force can be seen in the watch system. Men were paid to regularly patrol the streets according to set beats, and some wore uniforms. However, they were poorly paid and often of low status. They were not necessarily particularly well-respected, as there were concerns that they accepted bribes from those they were supposed to be policing, and were corrupt.

INVESTIGATIONS

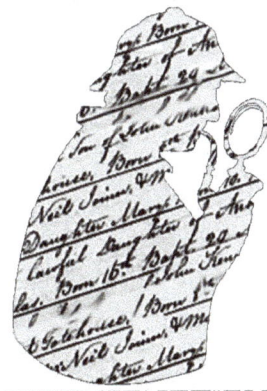

The victim, or judicial officers paid by the victim, conducted the investigations. Trials were victim led and the victim paid the costs of the trial and prosecution.

After the arrest, the victim either brought the felon to trial before a JP or magistrate, or agreed not to do so for compensation.

INCARCERATION AND TRIAL

The accused would be held in the local 'lock-up' until they could be examined by a magistrate.

The victim would have to produce the witnesses before a magistrate. At this time, statements would be made and signed. It was then up to the magistrate to decide what to do with the accused. At this point, depending upon the nature of the offence and the discretion of the parties involved, the accused might be tried "summarily" (i.e. without a jury) before the Justice of the Peace (JP) or forwarded on for indictment and jury trial, either at a Sessions of the peace, or at the Old Bailey.

It was for the grand jury to decide whether the prosecutor's case had sufficient grounds for it to proceed to a full trial before a petty jury, whose verdicts could determine whether the accused was found guilty, but also in determining the penal options available to the judges in sentencing the convict.

In some ways, the system for criminal prosecution was similar to our system of civil prosecution. Under both, it is the victim who ordinarily initiates and controls the process by which the offender is brought to justice. There is, however, at least one major difference between the two systems. In the modern civil case, if the victim succeeds in winning his case, the person he sued is required to pay him damages. In the 18th century, if the victim of a crime won his case, the criminal was hanged, transported, or possibly pardoned. Under the 18th century system of private criminal prosecution there seems to be no provision for damages to be awarded to the victim as a result of successful prosecution, therefore it was difficult to induce people to sue.

One solution was to establish substantial rewards for the conviction of criminals charged with particularly serious crimes. This led to new difficulties. In some cases, it was alleged that the accused were framed for offences. Other cases were said to be the result of entrapment; the perpetrators were persuaded to commit the crimes by those whose real purpose was to betray them for the reward.

The criminal justice system of the early nineteenth century was still fundamentally victim-led, with the responsibility of prosecution resting with the victim, although the magistrates and a developing police force increasingly were paid by the Crown.

In the event of a perceived crime, victims determined what came next. They could simply not report the offence at all, or if they did go to the trouble of detecting and apprehending the accused, they could either take the culprit before a justice of the peace (JP) or magistrate, or agree not to prosecute the individual in exchange for some form of compensation. At this point, depending upon the nature of the offence and the discretion of the parties involved, the accused might be tried "summarily" (i.e. without a jury) before the JP or magistrate, or forwarded on for indictment and jury trial, either at a Sessions of the Peace, or at the Old Bailey. It was for the grand jury to decide whether the prosecutor's case had sufficient grounds for it to proceed to a full trial before a petty jury, whose verdicts could determine whether the accused was found guilty, but also in determining the penal options available to the judges in sentencing the convict.

CRIMINAL COURTS SYSTEM

For most of the period of transportation to Australia, the criminal court system in England and Wales consisted of;

- ❧ Petty sessions where minor offences were dealt with by mostly unpaid, non-professional judges known as Justices of the Peace and, later in the period, paid Magistrates

- ❧ Quarter sessions were held four times a year and were also presided over by Justices of the Peace

- ❧ Assize courts where the more serious criminal trials tended to be heard, taking place at least twice a year and presided over by professional judges

- ❧ Court of King's Bench was a central royal court sitting at Westminster with an overriding jurisdiction over the other lower courts

The assizes heard criminal cases as well as cases passed on from the central Westminster courts. English and Welsh counties were grouped into assize 'circuits' where cases were heard:

- &o Home, Norfolk and South-Eastern Circuits
- &o Midland Circuit
- &o Northern and North-Eastern Circuits
- &o Oxford Circuit
- &o Welsh Circuits including Chester
- &o Western Circuit

JUSTICES OF THE PEACE

Justices of the Peace did not receive a wage from the government, but were entitled to charge small fees for their services.

The landed gentry typically took on the role. It was assumed that they did not depend on such payments, and thus dispensed justice without the incentive of financial gain.

The suspect would be brought before the justice in his parlour. There, the complaint would be heard, statements from the victim and any witnesses recorded, and a brief examination of the suspect taken as to whether they had anything to say in response to the charge.

If the JP concluded that no crime had in fact been committed, they could dismiss the case. If it was proved that a crime had been committed, he was obliged to commit the suspect for trial at the sessions of the peace or at the higher court of the Old Bailey, whether the evidence, either for or against the accused, was strong or weak.

In the late eighteenth century, there were complaints that the landed gentry was being replaced as JPs by corrupt "trading justices" - middle class men who treated the office simply as a source of income to be exploited. This bad reputation was mostly undeserved, but the complaints nonetheless led to the development of magistrates' and police courts which sought to remove the problem of JPs treating their work as a "business", and instead make the pre-trial process more consistent, efficient, fair and "professional".

MAGISTRATES' COURTS

In the late 18th and into the 19th Century, the system began to change. Magistrates' Courts were introduced.

The first of the magistrates' courts was created by the Court of Aldermen in the City of London (who had the powers of justices of the peace) in 1737. The aldermen now sat in rotation daily at the Guildhall, to hear cases from the western half of the City, with the Lord Mayor hearing cases from the eastern half at the Mansion House. The second such court was established in the 1750s at Bow Street in Westminster. In 1792 seven "public offices" were set up across London to supplement the work of Bow Street. Each office was assigned three paid justices and six constables. In 1800, an eighth office, the Thames River Police Office, was opened, with a wide jurisdiction for dealing with offences committed on the river and in the riverside area. In the 1820s and 1830s, the formation of the Metropolitan Police prompted changes. In 1839, the format of what were now called Police Courts, presided over by magistrates, was fixed. By the 1850s, there were thirteen police courts in London.

Individual magistrates heard a wide range of criminal accusations, and in the case of the increasing number of petty offences, they had the power to act on their own to determine guilt and to order punishments. Many criminal cases were judged by the magistrates' and police courts. In 1855 they heard over 77,000 cases summarily, and forwarded some 19,000 for trial at sessions and courts. In that year, only 1,232 defendants were tried at the Old Bailey.

ASSIZES

The Assize records and the records of the old Bailey are the ones most likely to hold your convict ancestors' records. The National Archives of the UK are the repository for the Assize records. Not all assize records have survived as the assize clerks sometimes destroyed them when they ran out of space. Earlier records are less likely to have been kept than later ones.

The records of the Old Bailey are best accessed through the *Old Bailey Online* website.

Assize records usually give details of the accused, including the name, occupation and place of abode of the accused. However, they can be unreliable as aliases were often used and other false details were given. The place of abode mentioned is often where the crime took place rather than where the accused lived. Assize records consist of;

Crown and gaol books also known as minute books or agenda books

The best place to begin a search in the assize records is in the Crown and gaol books, also known as minute books or agenda books. These usually list:

- names of the accused
- charges against the accused
- plea
- verdict
- sentence

There may be a separate series of minute books for offences such as the failure of local communities to keep local roads and bridges in a good state of repair.

Indictments

These are the formal statements of the charge against the accused, usually annotated with plea, verdict and sentence.

Each indictment usually gives:

- name of the defendant together with any aliases
- this or her occupation
- a parish of residence
- the date of the alleged offence (by regnal year)
- details of the alleged offence, together with the name of the victim
- a list of prosecution witnesses

The details of the defendant should be treated with caution, especially before the late 19th century. The defendant's occupation was normally given as 'labourer' and the parish of residence is invariably the parish in which the alleged offence took place. The alleged offence is defined by lengthy and formal phrases and some, especially in cases of serious misdemeanour, such as perjury or libel, are several membranes long.

Indictments were filed in large unwieldy bundles together with other related records, depending on the period and the circuit, such as those containing details of jury panels, coroners' inquisitions, examinations and depositions, gaol calendars, trial minutes, commissions, presentments of non-criminal offences and recognizances (which give names, parishes of residence and occupation and are usually far more accurate than those given on the indictments themselves).

Assize indictments in this period were either handwritten or partly printed and partly written on parchment.

Depositions and examinations

Depositions, sometimes known as sessions papers, consist of pre-trial witness statements. However, the survival rate for these records is relatively poor and those that do survive have been heavily weeded. Only depositions in capital cases, usually murder and riot, tend to survive.

Transcripts

Transcripts of what was actually said in court do not normally survive with the records held at The National Archives. A collection of contemporary pamphlet accounts of what was said in court during mostly celebrated trials for the period 1660-1908 is available on microfiche in the reading rooms at The National Archives. The *Old Bailey Online* website provides detailed proceedings (although not complete transcripts of what was said) for trials at the London central criminal court.

Other records

Other assize records can include:

- pleadings
- statements of claim, defence and counterclaim
- draft minutes of trials
- correspondence of the assize clerks, mostly administrative
- coroners' inquisitions
- jury lists
- financial business including fees and costs.

THE VOYAGE TO AUSTRALIA

The voyage to Australia on convict transport vessels is generally thought of as an horrendous experience. Of the 1017 convicts who came on the Second Fleet, arriving in Sydney in 1790, a quarter of them died at sea.

A third of the convicts from the 2nd Fleet died as a result of this disastrous and under resourced voyage.

However, the Second Fleet was an exception. Death rates on the first fleet were lower. Taking into account the scale of the operation, and the long sailing time involved, the European settlement of Australia can be seen as a highly successful logistical achievement.

This chart shows the monthly death rates on both the convict hulks and male convict vessels over time.

Starting prior to transportation to Australia in the 1770s, when there were convicts on hulks, it shows the death rate on the hulks, and the death rate on the convict voyages to Australia.

In the late 18th early 19th century these rates dropped considerably. The difference was made by the introduction of surgeon superintendents, trained by the British Navy, first into the hulks and then into the ships. They were introduced onto every single convict vessel, becoming mandatory after 1815.

Little was known about epidemics at this time. Most believed in the Miasma Theory of medicine, if it smelled bad then it was bad for you. They believed that disease was carried on and spread by foul-smelling air.

However, it was in a surgeon's best interests to land as many live convicts as possible. They received a bonus payment for doing so. If the death rate on a voyage was high, the surgeon had to provide an explanation. Bad reports could result in loss of money and a downgrading of their future employment prospects.

Every convict vessel surgeon was required to keep a journal. Many of these journals have survived and are kept in the ADM101 Series in the British Archives. (ADM is the code for Admiralty.) This list is available through the British National Archives http://search.ancestry.com.au/search/db.aspx?dbid=2318. The list also includes non-convict vessels.

On the right hand side of the landing page is a "browse this collection" box. Restrict your search to the ship on which you know that your convict ancestor sailed.

You may also find the surgeon and his records listed on Jen Willetts' Australian website;

Free Settler or Felon

http://www.jenwilletts.com.au

A word to the wise, you may not find your ancestor in the surgeon's journal.

Only those who were treated for illness, died or made their presence known individually to the surgeon will be recorded. The surgeon's record for an individual has the date admitted, the name of the patient, their age, their status - e.g. "convict" or "private 50th regiment", their diagnosis, the date they were discharged from the sick list and the outcome, including death.

However, surgeons' journals may also have much more detailed descriptions of the voyage than might be found elsewhere. Often, when a convict was put on the sick list, the surgeon included the latitude and longitude and sometimes the temperature and barometer readings. It's sometimes possible to plot the journey that the vessel took from the surgeon's journal.

Charles Bateson's book, *"The Convict Ships"*, is a great reference. It includes the tonnage of each ship, its insurance rating, where it was from, how many convicts on board and the duration of the voyage. It is also available on CD.

HOW DANGEROUS WAS THE VOYAGE FOR CONVICTS?

Surprisingly, it was twice as safe as travelling across the Atlantic to North America as a free passenger in the same period. This was mainly due to the hygiene methods that surgeons introduced on convict vessels. The decks were scrubbed, convicts were washed with seawater and their clothes were washed.

While surgeons didn't have the benefit of our modern understanding of hygiene and disease, all of these measures were quite effective.

Another reason for lower death rates was the introduction of pre-voyage checks. According to research carried out by the University of Tasmania, health screening of convicts prior to sailing cut the death rate from 4.4 deaths per thousand per month to 0.7.

Embarkation usually took four or five days. Surgeons were able to refuse to take anyone who was sick on embarkation and put them back on land before the ship sailed. Surgeons watched for signs of sickness amongst convicts after they'd been loaded and put on them land if they believed it was unlikely they would last the voyage. As well as not embarking people who were sick, most older convicts were not put on board the vessel.

There is clear evidence that the intervention of surgeons both in the hulks and on board the vessel made an important difference. There is a report on the hulk Leviathan available on Jen Willets website at *http://www.jenwillets.com/prison_hulk_report_1838.htm* that describes the daily routine put in place by the surgeon to combat illness and the spread of disease.

WHAT WERE THE CAUSES OF SICKNESS AND DEATH ON THE VOYAGE?

These are the most common diagnoses that resulted in death and that saw convicts admitted to sick bay.

- ‭ℬℴ‬ Diarrhoea and dysentery
- ℬℴ Digestive system
- ℬℴ Fever
- ℬℴ Respiratory system
- ℬℴ Tuberculosis
- ℬℴ Circulatory system
- ℬℴ Sexually transmitted diseases
- ℬℴ Nausea
- ℬℴ Skin diseases
- ℬℴ Mental illness and behavioural disorders
- ℬℴ Pregnancy, childbirth and the puerperium (childbed fever)
- ℬℴ Diseases of the eye and ear
- ℬℴ Diseases of the genito-urinary system
- ℬℴ Diseases of the nervous system
- ℬℴ Diseases of the blood
- ℬℴ Scurvy

The big killers on board were things connected with diarrhoea, dysentery and constipation. Respiratory diseases, particularly amongst male convicts were responsible for quite a few deaths.

Female convicts were much more likely to die of diarrhoea and dysentery related disorders. This may be as a result of the high number of children that were on board female vessels. It's very difficult to keep sanitary conditions, particularly when you have stormy weather in the southern oceans. It is believed that this is why female convict vessels were less hygienic than males. Interestingly, deaths by childbirth accounted for a minority of female deaths.

This also applies to scurvy on male vessels. Scurvy is caused by a lack of vitamin C.

As scurvy worsens there can be poor wound healing, personality changes, and finally after 8-12 weeks, death from infection or bleeding. It was an issue, but it wasn't by any means the largest cause of death.

Men were far more likely to be at risk of scurvy than women. It is believed that this is due to the differences in the pre-voyage diet. Men were confined on the hulks. The hulk diet had quite a lot of meat in it but very few vegetables. Women convicts were confined on land in a prison. The prison diet was the reverse, a lot of vegetables and not much meat. So while female convicts received fewer calories prior to transportation, they had diets which did not set them up for scurvy in the same way as male convicts.

FEMALE CONVICTS

The *Female Convicts Research Centre* has excellent coverage of the role of surgeons and their contribution to the welfare of female convicts. Look on their website at *https://www.femaleconvicts.org.au/convict-ships/the-ships-surgeons*

Female convicts who were transported with babies and small children kept them down below decks with them during the voyage.

There were no soldiers on female convict ships. The only successful mutiny attempt on a convict vessel happened on a female ship. Possibly the British Government was worried that female convicts might form relationships with their soldier guards, which would make taking over a vessel easier.

CHILD CONVICTS

A child who was arrested, tried as a criminal and sentenced to transportation travelled unaccompanied by an adult. The youngest child convict that we know of was 11 years old. Where possible, authorities tried to provide child convict vessels solely for their transport. If they weren't able to send them on a children-only vessel, they would try and keep the children separate from the rest of the convicts on board. Child convicts were educated as part of their servitude, so that all of the children had some schooling. There were classes and different forms of education provided by the Government as well. There are 6 videos available on YouTube, created by Living Museums in Sydney that give insight into the lives of child convicts. A YouTube search of 'Child Convicts NSW' will find them.

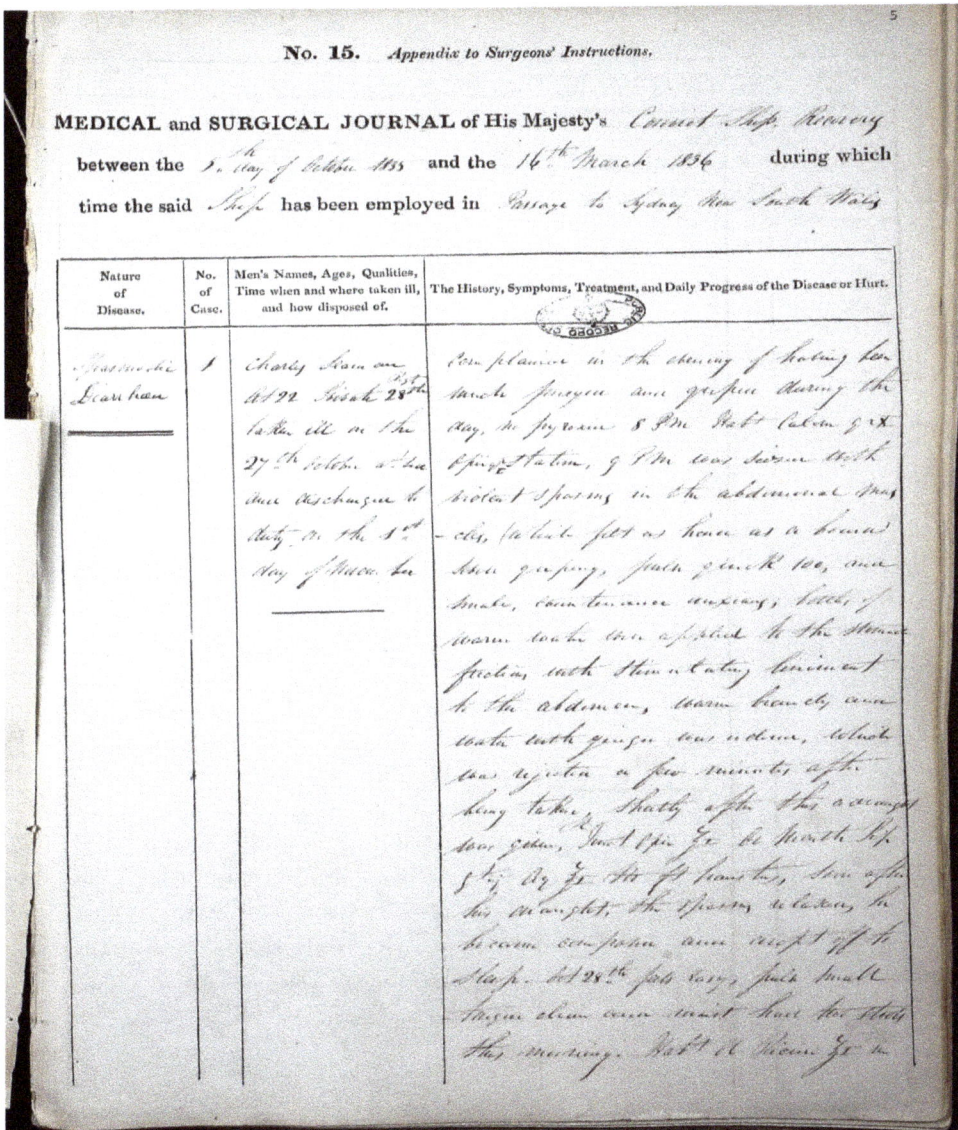

WHAT HAPPENED TO CONVICTS ON ARRIVAL IN AUSTRALIA?

Arrangements varied over time and between colonies. In the early days there were few public buildings and few means to process new arrivals. Paper was scarce and for this reason alone the colonial administration was unable to keep the kind of detailed record keeping systems that were in common use later on.

Before the construction of Barracks and Female Factories in Sydney, Parramatta and Hobart most convicts were left to their own devices. The hours they worked for government had to be limited, as convicts needed to earn sufficient money elsewhere to pay rent for lodgings, although in most cases their rations and clothes were supplied from the colony stores.

This changed with the opening of Hyde Park Barracks in 1819. Paper became freely available and a new system of record keeping was introduced. From 1816 onwards convicts were described in increasing detail following disembarkation. Family history researchers are fortunate in that convicts became amongst the best documented citizens of the British Empire.

Important records were compiled after disembarkation. The most important of these, and the main record group for convicts arriving in NSW, was the Indent. The word indent is itself revealing. It is derived from indenture.

An Indent is a legal document assigning to the ship's captain property rights, or "ownership" of the labour of the convict for the duration of the voyage.

After arrival in Australia those property rights were signed over to the Colonial Government. Some Indents are more detailed than others.

In the 1830s, the indents for NSW were printed which makes them much easier to read.

THE BARRACKS

In Van Diemen's Land, male convicts landed in Hobart were first sent to the Hobart Penitentiary to await details of to whom they would be assigned or to which government work gang they would be sent.

In NSW, male convicts landed in Port Jackson were sent to Hyde Park Barracks for assignment.

The landing processes would have included having hair closely cropped and being kitted out with new work clothing. This tended to be issued from the store as and when available. Convicts did not wear a uniform.

On arrival, male convicts were assigned to work. Some were sent to be agricultural labourers or house servants and workers on properties owned by settlers or Ticket of Leave convicts.

Others were employed in their trades; gardeners, bakers, cooks, builders, carpenters, on government work sites or in the Barracks. Those who were considered hardened criminals or in need of further severe punishment were assigned to government hard labour on road gangs. They were housed in the Barracks if the works site was close enough, or in stockades wherever the road gang was working.

For those housed in Hyde Park Barracks, life was miserable and fraught with danger of illness, injury and death.

The main meal of the day was a fatty, salty stew, made with fresh beef and a quarter of an ounce of salt for each man, and a few vegetables. Each day, the rations were carted into the barracks, and the storekeeper stacked the sacks and crates onto the shelves in his store. He was also kept busy, day and night, protecting the stores from hordes of rats. A storekeeper once reported he had killed 352 rats in one month![1]

Sleeping conditions in the Barracks were appalling and overcrowded. Beneath the floorboards of the dormitories, hundreds of rats made nests, drawn to the warmth and scraps of bread stashed away by convicts.

---

1   *Hyde Parks Barracks Museum https:// sydneylivingmuseums.com.au/convict-sydney/day-life-convict*

The roof leaked, dripping all night on the sleepers below, and many of the hammocks were filthy. The glass in the windows was broken, and the heat in the summer and cold in the winter filled the buildings.

During the "icy winter" of 1836, on June 28th, the thousands of convicts in Hyde Park awoke to snow "nearly an inch deep". "About seven o'clock in the morning a drifting fall covered the streets," The Sydney Herald reported at the time. "A razor-keen wind from the west blew pretty strongly at the time, and all together, it was the most English like winter morning … ever experienced."

The Sydney Monitor, reported: "We believe snow was never seen in Sydney before the previous night." The meteorological table in The Sydney Herald recorded that, on the morning of the snow, the temperature dropped to three degrees Celsius (or 38 degrees Fahrenheit).

The convicts' day started with breakfast in the mess halls. Then, already weary from a night spent in close confinement on hammocks in a rat infested barracks, government convicts marched out every morning after muster.

For most, the work was dreary, back-breaking and hazardous. For convicts assigned to work gangs outside the barracks, conditions were no easier.

Stockades were built in areas, such as Wollongong and along the Paddy's river where the Great Northern Road was under construction.

In May 1839, Lady Jane Franklin visited the convict stockade at Wollongong.

In her diary she described the living conditions of the convict labour force.

"The barracks and huts of the prisoners are here. We looked into the huts, etc. There are about 115 convicts here and about 30 troops of the 80th Regiment. Captain Rait is the Commandant. The men are lodged in wooden 'boxes' forming the side of a square on the tongue of land which was the only part Sir Richard Bourke would accept from Mr Smith. There are 5 or 6 of these 'boxes', with no windows, and holding 24 each.

No light or air enters them but from iron bars at the top of the door. Men were lying on the bare floors and on bare wooden platforms alone. We were told they were locked in only at night, but found them locked in now. We saw no mattresses. 'Have they none?' We asked the soldiers. 'Only the sick', was their reply."

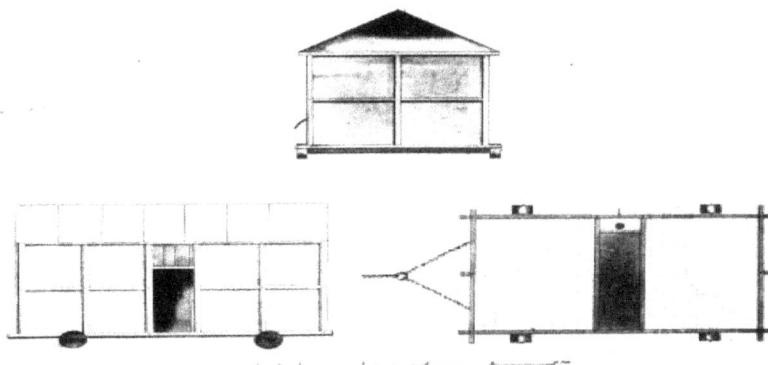

Sketch of a Portable Wooden House to contain Twenty Ironed Ganged Convicts No date

THE FEMALE FACTORIES

Female Factories were the equivalent of prisons for female convicts. They were also the place where female convicts were taken when they disembarked from the vessel. They were housed there while the colonial government decided where they were going to be assigned. There were 13 female factories - Parramatta (2), Bathurst, Newcastle, Port Macquarie (2), Moreton Bay (2), Hobart Town, Georgetown, Cascades, Launceston and Ross

Female convicts landed in Hobart were walked through the streets to the Cascade Female Factory. You can find out more about the Cascade Female Factory through the website of the Female Convict Research Centre *http://www.femaleconvicts.org.au/index.php/convict-institutions/female-factories/cascades-ff*

Female convicts landed in Sydney were sent by boat up the Parramatta River to the Parramatta Female Factory to await news of how they would be disposed.

There is a very good website on Parramatta Female Factory at

http://www.parragirls.org.au/female-factory.php

UNDER THE EYE OF GOVERNMENT

On Sundays, all convicts had to attend church services. From Hyde Park Barracks, the Protestants crossed the road to St James' Church, while the Catholics marched down to St Mary's Chapel. Ticket-of-leave holders and married convicts living outside the barracks were also required to attend.

Once their Ticket-of-leave was granted convicts could work for pay in a specified place. Life was less regulated, although certain rules such as Church attendance and Permission to Marry still applied.

It was only after they received a Certificate of Freedom or Pardon that a convict's life became, almost, their own.

Those with a *Conditional* Pardon were forbidden ever to return to Britain. Should they do so, the original sentence would immediately be imposed. For many, this would have meant hanging.

Once a convict landed in Australia, records were kept of where they disembarked, to whom they were assigned, how they came here. Every move a convict made right up to their certificate of freedom was recorded. Each record tells you where to look next, giving Family Historians a rich source of information on which to build their convict ancestor's story.

CONVICT RECORDS

When searches of vital records fail to reveal the arrival date of an ancestor, there can be a very good reason. They may have been transported to Australia as a convict.

Ask yourself the following questions;

- ∽ Was my ancestor a convict?
- ∽ If so, what was their crime?
- ∽ Where and when were they tried and convicted?
- ∽ What was her/his sentence?
- ∽ How did they come to Australia?
- ∽ Where did they land?
- ∽ What happened after they arrived?

NSW, Qld and Tasmania have the most convict records, with Tasmania having rich sources of information for early convicts and for Van Diemen's Land.

NSW State Archives and Records

There are comprehensive guides to searching the archive's records online at the NSW State Archives and Records website.

Go to the website, look down the home page and click the picture labelled Convicts.

Popular

Census and Musters

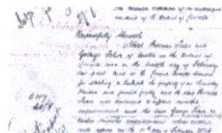
Colonial Secretary

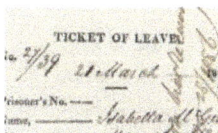
Convicts

Divorce

Immigration and Shipping

Start by searching the Convict databases in the NSW State Archives. A single searchable database of 140,000+ entries contains;
- ဢ certificates of freedom
- ဢ bank accounts
- ဢ deaths
- ဢ exemptions from Government Labor
- ဢ pardons
- ဢ tickets of leave and
- ဢ tickets of leave passports.

If you select *Search the Index* and *Convicts*, the Convict Index search screen will open.

You do not need to fill in anything but your ancestor's name, then click submit. If any records are found, a list will be displayed.

If you find a record for your ancestor, you will then have to order and pay for a copy of the record.

About Us   Archives   Government Recordkeeping   Government Records Repository

NSW GOVERNMENT | **State Archives & Records**

Archives / Collection & Research / Research A-Z / Online Indexes

Convict Index

Surname

Firstname

Alias

Remarks

Select record type

Vessel

Year

yyyy

[Submit]   Reset

Order copies of the records

Once you have located an entry of interest from our Indexes, select the checkbox under the 'Add to Cart' column at the left of screen. Click either on one of the 'Add to Cart' buttons, or if you have finished all your selections, the 'Proceed to Checkout' button. Review your selections in the Cart screen. Click on the 'Proceed' button when you are ready to enter your delivery and payment details.

SUCCESSFUL SEARCHING

The less you know about your convict ancestor the more difficult the search can be. Here are some hints to help.

NAMES

&∞ Use the wildcard character - % or * - It can represent any character in a keyword. For example:

&∞ *Smith%* will return all entries that start with 'Smith', whereas

&∞ *%Smith%* will return any entries that have 'Smith' somewhere in the name (such as 'Shoesmith')

&∞ *%Sm%t* will return any entries that have 'Smith' somewhere in the name as well as other names such as 'Charlesmouth', 'Osmont', 'Portsmouth', 'Smallworth', 'Smeaton', 'Smart', Smythe' or 'Smithers'.

PLACES

&∞ The wildcard character is also very useful when searching for an entry by an option other than surname. For instance, a search of *%Windsor%* in a locality or description field will find the word 'Windsor' anywhere in that field.

&∞ *M%Brook* in a locality or description field will find the word 'Muswellbrook', 'Muscellbrook', 'MuscleBrook' and 'Wollombi Brook'.

SEARCH FOR MORE THAN ONE NAME

&∞ Simply enter each name separated by a comma. No spaces. For example: *Porter, Newton'* in the Surname field will return all entries with the surnames Porter and Newton.

There are other NSW Archives searches besides the Convict Index possible. Go to Census and Musters in the NSW Convicts archives. There are four databases;

&∞ The Blue Book 1822 - 1857 - this is the returns of the colony. A statistical document and extremely interesting.

&∞ Census 1841, which is indexed but not digitised.

&∞ Census 1891

&∞ Census 1901

TASMANIA

Tasmania has a wealth of Convict records, not all of which are available through Ancestry. The Tasmanian State Government's LINC website, *https://www.linc.tas.gov.au/family-history/Pages/Convict-life.aspx* contains Tasmanian convict records, including the NSW convict records.

BEYOND TRANSPORTATION RECORDS

The British Government transported about 76,000 convicts to Tasmania between 1804 and 1853. You can search for them online.

Once convicts arrived in Australia, the Hyde Park Barracks authorities kept very careful records on their movements and their life. There are records of the work they were assigned to, the name of any settler to whom they were assigned as workers, if and when they were given a ticket of leave or pardon.

Convicts had to request permission of the authorities to marry and there is a register of "Convict Permissions to Marry", searchable online.

Of course, if you have a subscription to Ancestry.com.au, or access through the local library to the Ancestry Library Edition, most of the convict records of Australia are available to you as part of your subscription and a single search will find records from the various indexes they hold.

In some cases, the Ancestry search will also show you a digitised copy of the original record. This can be then downloaded to your computer or saved to your ancestor's record.

Once you have confirmed that your ancestor was a convict, you will also want to know how they fell into crime, what their crime was and more about his/her life before they arrived in Australia.

You may have an idea of the crime for which they were convicted and transported, possibly the assizes or court in which they were tried and some idea of their occupation, if any, prior to their crime. If not, then following the principle of working backwards, examine the documents that you have already.

If you have found a muster, or a Ticket of Leave, or Permission to Marry, you will find the name of the ship they arrived on.

You may find the ship's Convict Indent. If so, you will have the best possible description of your convict ancestor. Opposite, you will see an page from the Convict Indent of the convict ship Recovery, 1843.

The indent is a list of all convicts aboard. It gives you;

- 🕮 each convict's prisoner number,
- 🕮 indent number,
- 🕮 name,
- 🕮 age,

- 🕮 education,
- 🕮 religion,
- 🕮 marital status,
- 🕮 children,
- 🕮 native place,
- 🕮 trade or calling, offence,
- 🕮 trial place and date,
- 🕮 sentence,
- 🕮 any former conviction,
- 🕮 height,
- 🕮 complexion, colour of hair and eyes and
- 🕮 any particular marks, such as scars.

There are also Colonial History columns for dates to be added later. These are the dates on which they received any Colonial Sentence, Ticket of Leave, Pardon, and/or Certificate of Freedom, or the date they died or left the Colony.

From the indent came the information that led us to finding the details of Edmund (*note the difference in spelling on the indent*) Collins' offence and trial in the Northamptonshire newspapers of the time.

This first account gave us the crime and initial judgement of death.

The second told us of the reduction in the sentence to transportation for 14 years. It also identified the hulk on which Edmund was imprisoned.

However, not all trials were recorded and not all assizes and court records can be accessed online.

The following convicts were removed from our county gaol, yesterday se'nnight, in order to be put on board the Leviathan Hulk, at Portsmouth. John Haynes, Joseph Russell, Thomas Steanes, and Samuel Dawes, under sentence of transportation for life; James Short, George Cox, William Moyses, Joseph Calcutt, Norman Smith, the younger, Edmund Collins, James Turner, William Brown, for fourteen years; John Lane and Geo. Taylor, for seven years.

The British Newspapers Archive, https://www. britishnewspaperarchive.co.uk, is a good place to start when you can't find a record of the trial..

Judgment of Death was recorded against Edmund Collins, aged 18, *James Turner*, aged 36, and *Wm. Brown*, aged 20, for having robbed Joseph York of £3. 15s. on the highway, at Dodford.

Thomas Dodson, aged 46, was acquitted on a charge of stealing a half-crown, belonging to Samuel Bull, of Cottingham.

George Taylor, aged 22, a sheep-stealer, was sentenced to seven years' transportation.

(54)

NEW SOUTH WALES, 1836.

ALEXANDER NEILL, Surgeon Superintendent, arrived from ENGLAND, 25th February, 1836.

(53)

LIST of MALE CONVICTS, by the Ship RECOVERY (3). THOMAS JOHNSON, Master,

It requires a subscription, but has a pay as you go option that makes it affordable. A word of caution, don't take the PAYG option until you know exactly what you are looking for.

Membership of the Australian National Library also gives you access to the British Newspaper Archives. The search is a little more difficult but the cost is nil.

If you know on which ship your ancestor sailed, search the records for that ship's list and date of sailing.

A useful place to search for convict ships and their records is the Convict Records website.

https://convictrecords.com.au/ships.

All ships are listed in alphabetical order and for each ship there is a list of the sailing dates and a clickable link to information, including the ships captain, surgeon etc.

After you have the details of crime and trial, and if newspaper reports provide other background information, you may go where your curiosity takes you. In my case, further research into the hulk *Leviathan* revealed a Chief Surgeon's report on the *Leviathan* containing details of the prisoners' daily life on board and the conditions under which they were held. I now had a very good insight into what Ned's life would have been like once he turned convict.

Turning back to a convict's arrival in Australia, there are various records and research tools that can be used to follow your ancestor through his/her Australian life.

The musters will give you the place to which he/she has been sent and the job to which they have been assigned. This could be to a particular person, as a servant or farm worker, or it could be to 'government'.

If 'government', then he was probably assigned to hard labour or to some other useful task within a government body.

For example, Hyde Park Barracks was where many government convicts were housed while they were working on road gangs and government public works.

The Barracks also had their own convict assignees; cooks, stores labourers, carpenters. Convicts who had a trade were in high demand. However, anyone with a life sentence, or a serious crime on their record, was most likely to spend a long period at hard labour before being allowed to take up their trade again.

A search of the people or site to which a convict was assigned can give you a good picture of their life. Many convicts worked on road gangs at Paddy's River. This was an important and fascinating project in Australia's early history, building the Great Northern Road. Convicts were assigned to properties and houses of famous people.

Once a convict gained a Ticket of Leave (TOL) they were free to work for pay within a set district, but a record was kept of their whereabouts and to move to another area required permission.

Examine the TOL on p60. At the bottom '*allowed to remain in the District of Campbelltown*' was noted in 1844 when the TOL was granted. On the side is a note that states '*altered to Goulburn 1847*'. A Ticket of Leave and Pardon can help you track a convict's movements through the colony.

COLONIAL SECRETARY'S RECORDS

There are references to individual convicts in the correspondence that went through the Colonial Secretary's Office. Petitions for marriages or for their families to join them, assignments of workers and servants to landowners, misdemeanours, all went through the correspondence. It is indexed and available through the NSW State Archives. There are a number of webcasts to help you navigate the indices.

TROVE

There are newspapers and Gazettes in the Trove collection that yield insights into a convict's life in Australia. Local papers have sports articles. Your convict could have been a whizz at cricket and the star batsman on the village team.

A name search through Trove reveals stories of an individual convict's life in the colony; births, deaths and marriages, business classifieds and reports of accidents or events can all help to build the picture of your convict ancestor's participation in the history of Australia.

Here are two items from Trove that solved the mystery of why our convict ancestor moved from Campbelltown to Goulburn, set up what looked to be a return to his calling as baker, yet within a year moved back to Campbelltown.

May 1849

EDMUND COLLINS,
PASTRY-COOK,
CONFECTIONER,
Fancy Bread and Biscuit Baker,
SLOANE STREET,
NEAR MR. MANDELSON'S HOTEL, GOULBURN.

BEGS leave to inform the inhabitants of the surrounding districts, that he has removed to the above commodious premises, where he is prepared to supply

Every Article in the Confectionary line
EQUAL TO THE BEST HOUSES IN
SYDNEY AND LONDON.

Lozenges one shilling per pound
Common Sweetmeats nine pence per ditto
Cordials of every description at six shillings per gal.
First quality Biscuit eighteen shillings per cwt.
☞ Wedding and Christening Cakes at the shortest Notice.

June 1849

SHOOTING THE MOON—On Thursday night, a tenant of Mr. Mandelson's named Collins, who was carrying on business as Baker and Confectioner, in Sloane-street, took a sudden departure from his premises with his wife and child, goods and all. The most important part of the "flit" is, that in the hurry of moving, Collins forgot to settle a few accounts due by him to some of the trades-people in the town. Singular to relate, the last tenant in the same house left Goulburn in a similar manner.

Sad but true, Ned had a penchant for having good ideas implemented in the wrong place at the wrong time. Now we know where this family trait came from.

As an example of a convict records trail, working backwards from the first record found, in *Convicts Permissions to Marry*, the research in understanding the life of Ned Collins was as follows;

- Convict muster for the 'Recovery.'
- Indent for the 'Recovery' - this gave an inordinate amount of detail for Ned; crime, place of trial, literacy, occupation, his physical description including tattoos and scars.
- Northampton newspapers for the account of the trial and details of the crime, which also named the hulk that he was on while he awaited embarkation to NSW.

Forward from disembarkation, the research trail was;

- Musters
- Church Record of marriage
- Births of Children
- Ticket of Leave and Pardon
- Trove

From there, the trail led us through the history of Australia's growth to nationhood, through depression to the Gold Rush, and on to Federation.

Simmons, Miner's Agent & Family, Gulgong, NSW. Circa 1873

State Library NSW

CONVICT REFERENCES

There is a wealth of information available in NSW and Tasmania to assist you to identify and trace the life of a convict ancestor.

By far the best source of links to convict records is The Digital Panopticon: Tracing London Convicts in Britain and Australia, 1780-1925, (www.digitalpanopticon.org, last accessed June 2020)

The Digital Panopticon website allows you to search millions of records from around fifty datasets, relating to the lives of 90,000 convicts from the Old Bailey, to search individual convict life archives, explore and visualise data, and to learn more about crime and criminal justice in the past. This resource and reference list is just a beginning.

1. Australian Government. "Convicts and the British Colonies in Australia." Convicts and the British colonies in Australia, 2017.

2. Barbara Turner. "Australia's First Fleet." Accessed December 7, 2018. http://members.pcug.org.au/~pdownes/dps/1stflt.htm.

3. Barbara Turner. "Australia's Second Fleet." Accessed December 7, 2018. http://members.pcug.org.au/~pdownes/dps/2ndflt.htm.

4. "Convicts | NSW State Archives." Accessed December 4, 2018. https://www.records.nsw.gov.au/archives/collections-and-research/guides-and-indexes/convicts.

5. Cora Num. "CoraWeb - Convicts." Accessed December 4, 2018. http://www.coraweb.com.au/categories/convicts.

6. Cyndi Ingle. "Cyndi's List - Australia - Convicts, Prisons, Prisoners; Outlaws." Accessed December 7, 2018. https://www.cyndislist.com/australia/convicts/.

7. "Female Convicts Research Centre." Accessed December 7, 2018. https://www.femaleconvicts.org.au/.

8. Foxhall, Katherine. "From Convicts to Colonists: The Health of Prisoners and the Voyage to Australia, 1823-53." Journal of Imperial and Commonwealth History, 2011. https://doi.org/10.1080/03086534.2011.543793.

9. Government of Western Australia State Records. "Convict Records | SRO." Accessed December 4, 2018. http://www.sro.wa.gov.au/archive-collection/collection/convict-records.

10. Jaunay, Graham. "Graham Jaunay - Australian Ancestral & Local History Researcher Helping You with Your Genealogy and Family History." Accessed December 3, 2018. http://www.jaunay.com/.

11. Jill Chambers. "Black Sheep Search - Home." Accessed December 7, 2018. https://www.black-sheep-search.co.uk/.

12. Karskens, Grace. "The Convict Road Station Site at Wisemans Ferry: An Historical and Archaeological Investigation." Australian Historical Archaeology, 1984.

13. Kercher, Bruce. "Perish or Prosper: The Law and Convict Transportation in the British Empire, 1700-1850." Law and History Review, 2003. https://doi.org/10.2307/3595119.

14. Lesley Uebel & Hawkesbury on the Net. "Claim A Convict." Accessed December 7, 2018. http://www.hawkesbury.net.au/claimaconvict/index.php.

15. Libraries Tasmania. "Convicts." Accessed December 4, 2018. https://libraries.tas.gov.au/convict-portal/Pages/convicts.aspx.

16. Marion Purnell. "Australian Royalty - Australian Royalty: A Family Tree of Colonial Australians, Their Forbears and Descendants." Accessed December 4, 2018. https://australianroyalty.net.au/index.php.

17. National Library of Australia. "Convicts | National Library of Australia." Accessed December 4, 2018. https://www.nla.gov.au/research-guides/convicts.

18. Nelson, Rob, and Joan O'Donovan. "Convicts To Australia - A Guide to Researching Your Convict Ancestors," 2000. http://members.iinet.net.au/~perthdps/convicts/index.html.

19. Nicholas, Stephen. Convict Workers: Reinterpreting Australia's Past. Australian Studies, 1988.

20. Oxley, Deborah. Convict Maids: The Forced Migration of Women to Australia. Studies in Australian History, 1996.

21. Queensland Family History Society Technology Advisory Group. QFHS. "Queensland Family History Society." Accessed December 3, 2018. https://www.qfhs.org.au/.

22. Reid, Kirsty. "Setting Women to Work: The Assignment System and Female Convict Labour in Van Diemen's Land, 1820-1839." Australian Historical Studies, 2003. https://doi.org/10.1080/10314610308596234.

23. Robbins, William Murray. "Management and Resistance in the Convict Work Gangs, 1788-1830." Journal of Industrial Relations, 2003. https://doi.org/10.1111/1472-9296.00088.

24. State Library of Queensland; "British Convict Transportation Registers Database." Accessed December 7, 2018. http://www.slq.qld.gov.au/resources/family-history/convicts.

25. State Library of Queensland. "Family History." Accessed December 3, 2018. http://www.slq.qld.gov.au/resources/family-history.

26. Steve Thomas. "Convict Records of Australia." Accessed December 4, 2018. https://convictrecords.com.au/.

27. Tranter, Bruce, and Jed Donoghue. "Convict Ancestry: A Neglected Aspect of Australian Identity." Nations and Nationalism, 2003. https://doi.org/10.1111/1469-8219.00127.

ADD YOUR OWN REFERENCES HERE

EMIGRATION

19TH CENTURY EMIGRATION

An emigrant is a person who is leaving one country to live in another.

An immigrant is a person who is entering a country from another to make a new home.

A refugee is a person who has fled to a new country because of a fear of losing their life.

The difference between an emigrant and a refugee lies in the motive behind the move and the intention to stay.

Emigrants move to another country to find a better life. They want to leave and look forward to moving. Their intention is to establish a new and better life in another place and to remain there for life. Immigration is controlled by laws in the country they are leaving and in the country to which they emigrating.

Refugees, on the other hand, leave their homeland because they fear for their lives. They are compelled to leave, often without thought or preparation. When they reach safety, there may not be the intention to stay. Many refugees have a strong desire to return to their homeland when it is safe to do so.

Whether emigrants or refugees, tracing our ancestors as they move from place to place usually involves searching through records from more than one country.

Records of emigrants are far easier to find than those of refugees, particularly when the refugees have fled violence and war. In wartime, records are destroyed or damaged, people leave in haste without taking any documents with them and enter across borders without the creation of official records of who they are and where they originated. For example, thousands of Jewish people were moved across Europe into camps between 1935 and 1946 and then made their way out of Europe to the USA, Australia and the Middle East following World War 2. Destruction of the camp and other records make tracing families so difficult that organisations have been created dedicated solely for the purpose of assisting those seeking information.

This book focuses on migration from Great Britain to Australia and other colonies during the late 17th, the 19th and 20th Centuries.

WHY EMIGRATE?

Why did so many people leave their homelands? The voyage to Australia sometimes took 17 weeks. Ships that crossed the oceans to Canada and Australia were small and the journey was very uncomfortable and dangerous. Why did so many leave?

People emigrate for reasons of religion, economics, politics and lifestyle.

Religion

Some of the first immigrants, particularly to the Americas, left as a result of *religious persecution*. This happened in Germany, France, Spain and England. One of the first religious emigrations was the voyage of the famous 'Mayflower' taking Quakers, known as the Pilgrim Fathers to the west coast of America.

American War of Independence

By the time the *American War of Independence* ended in 1783, the cost to the Great Britain was enormous. When the British soldiers returned from war many were reinstated in the jobs they had left, those who has taken their place on farms and in industry were forced to join the ranks of the unemployed.

French Revolution

In 1789 *the French Revolution* began and lasted for 10 years. Large numbers of French refugees moved to Britain, placing a strain on the economy and again taking work from local people or seeking financial assistance from the state.

The French Revolutionary War from 1793-1815 continued the drain on resources.

The Potato Famine

In the early 1800s *the Potato Famine* in Ireland and Scotland brought starvation to thousands of poor families. Industrialisation increased rapidly, so that prosperity passed by the ordinary pastoral and cottage industry labourer. Bad harvests led to an agricultural depression. The Corn Laws, tariffs and other trade restrictions on imported food and grain ("corn"), were passed to keep grain prices high to favour domestic producers.

As a result;

- food prices rose
- wages fell
- starvation set in.
- relief for the poor became urgent and in 1834 new Poor Laws led to the rise of Workhouses.

The Highland Clearances

In Scotland, *the Highland Clearances* began. Landowners in the Highlands and Outer Hebrides realised that they could gain more from farming sheep or cattle than they would ever collect in rents from their tenants.

Landlords evicted thousands of families, burning their cottages and establishing large sheep farms. Some of the evicted tenants were resettled in coastal crofts, often on very poor land. They were forced to subsist by collecting and smelting kelp, an occupation that was foreign to them.

Other crofters were employed in fishing for herring. The decline of the kelp and fishing industries, falling cattle prices, and, when potato blight hit, about 1846, the crofters were financially devastated. Disease and starvation spread.

Others, particularly in the Outer Hebrides and parts of Ireland, were forcibly removed by their landlords, loaded into ships and sent to Canada.

The numbers of McNeils found in the current telephone and professional directories of Nova Scotia (New Scotland) are testament to how many crofters and fishers from the island of Barra suffered this fate.

The European Depression of the 1840s

In the 1840s an *economic depression* hit. British workers living in France, employed on railway construction in the north, flax spinning and linen weaving in Lille and in a thriving lacemaking trade in Calais, were all taking work from French citizens.

Following local riots, eviction from their homes and angry cries of "*Allez les Anglais!*", they were forced to leave with but two options, the workhouses of England or emigration to the colonies. There was so much pressure on the Parishes, who bore the costs of the Workhouses, that officials began encouraging tradesmen, agricultural labourers and any who had skills to offer to the colonies, to emigrate. At the same time, the settlements in Australia were becoming well established. NSW needed farmers, builders and tradesmen. The few free settlers that were already in the Colony were lobbying for less transportation and more immigration to bring a balance to the population.

People arrived and remained in Australia for various reasons between 1777 and the 1850s.

- Convicts
- Free Settlers there was a trickle at first which increased during Macquarie's time.
- Soldiers and Marines, some of whom settled when their service time was up
- The Government Schemes - 1822-1830 and 1837-1840
- The Bounty Immigrants Scheme 1835-1841
- The Assisted Immigrants Scheme in the 1840s and 1850s
- The Gold Rush 1851

Following the two World Wars of the 20th Century, migration to Australia was actively promoted through such schemes as "Bring Out a Britain" in order to build a viable, predominately British population. When the Snowy Mountains Scheme and the Australian mineral resources and manufacturing industries demanded a larger workforce, European migration boomed. Australia became a multi-cultural society. This has continued into the 21st century with the influx of migrants and refugees following the Vietnam War and conflicts in Africa and the Middle East.

AUSTRALIAN IMMIGRATION

Between 1788 and 1868 approximately 160,000 convicts were sent to Australia. The first non-convict settlers were the military personnel who came with them as their guards and as administration for the Colony, their wives and children. The first free settlers, five single men and two families, arrived in 1793. The number of free settlers steadily grew, as did the number of native born people and convicts who had served their time and were now free citizens.

In the early days of the colony, NSW needed immigrants. Labour, skilled tradesmen, female domestic staff and farm servants were in short supply in the growing settlement. Attracting the right kind of settlers was difficult. It was cheaper and quicker for those wanting to emigrate to the 'new world' to travel to America. To attract immigrants to Australia, the Government needed to provide free or heavily subsidised passages. Assisted Immigrants were those who had all or part of their passage paid through three types of subsidy;

- Government assisted immigration, usually funded through the sale of government land,
- Bounty or
- Assistance through another scheme.

From 1815 the Colonial Government decided to encourage immigration of free settlers. Squatters leases were limited to 14 years.

The Colonial Government assisted some migrants by paying their fare to Australia and helped to set up farms and businesses alongside wealthy squatters.

About a third of free settlers who came to Australia between 1830 and 1850 paid their own fare. Convicts and settlers who came to Australia found that in comparison to the life they had left behind conditions were very good. Hard work and persistence had its rewards. They encouraged their relatives in England to come to Australia.

Women migrants were also assisted to come and work as domestic servants and to encourage marriages and childbirth. There was a need to balance the gender population.

Immigration schemes resulted in 58,000 people

coming to Australia between 1815 and 1840. Assisted immigration started in 1828. People were invited to apply for all or part of the cost of their passage.

In order to ensure that the colony received the right kind of immigrants, those who would fulfill the roles that it needed, there were some conditions such as age restrictions and "suitability" – young, healthy & useful with work experience. As a result, the Immigration Board lists show age, literacy, occupation etc

Assisted immigrants were supposed to pay back their passage money from the salary they received after arrival, but many refused.

68

BOUNTY IMMIGRATION

Eventually, in 1836, the government introduced a free assistance scheme called the Bounty system. It was aimed at bringing mechanics, tradesmen or agricultural labourers, farm servants and domestic servants to the colony. Character references were required. There were still age, occupational criteria, a requirement for testimonials (references) as well as a limit to number of children that could come with a family. Individuals or small groups could be sponsored by people in Australia.

Bounty ships were chartered by an agent in the UK. To fill the ship, prospective immigrants applied to the agent for inclusion. They were interviewed by the Immigration Board and, if deemed suitable, a Bounty was paid to the Agent.

Conditions were imposed upon Agents also. No payment would be made for people found to be unfit on arrival, too old or for any immigrant who died on the voyage.

Private employers who nominated individuals as immigrants also received subsidies.

- £30 for a man and wife under 30 years
- £15 for each single female 15y to 30y with the approval of the settler or the agent, and under the protection of a married couple or to stay with the family until otherwise provided for.
- £10 for each unmarried male 18y to 30y
- £5 for each child over 1 year of age.

PRIVATE SCHEMES

Private immigration schemes were introduced by Edward Gibbon Wakefield, Caroline Chisolm and John Dunmore Lang that provided free passage for specific groups of immigrants.

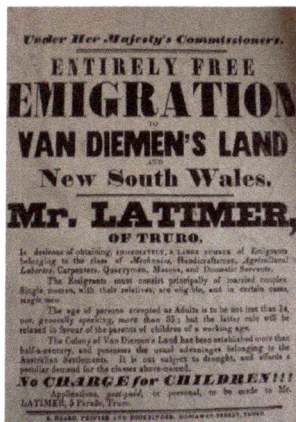

CAROLINE CHISOLM

Caroline Chisolm supported passages for emancipists' wives on 2 ships & for children on another.

She couldn't get official backing for this, so set up her own scheme of family emigration – The Family Colonization Loan Society in 1849. The Society received the savings of intending emigrants and loaned them the balance of the passage money.

JOHN DUNMORE LANG

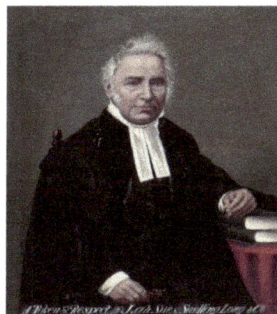

Lang was a Scottish Presbyterian Minister who arrived in NSW in 1824.

He was in England in 1830 to promote education and, struck by the numerous poor he found there, thought emigration could help them and produce moral reform in NSW.

Lang selected about 140 people, mostly Scottish tradesmen and their families, who could help build a college in Australia.

Their fare was to be repaid out of wages earned while building the college. He later proposed that reputable migrants who paid their own fare should receive a free grant of land.

He brought out 270 migrants on the Fortitude in 1848, but they received no land. He brought out 5 more ships with a total of 1200 migrants to Sydney, Port Phillip & Moreton Bay, including Lutherans from Germany.

The Highlands and Islands Emigration Society ran from 1852-1857, bringing 4910 men, women & children from Western Isles & Western Highlands. Most were families, with restrictions on the age and number of children. These emigrants paid a deposit & were loaned the balance from money provided by benefactors. Australian agents found them employment and collected the repayment of the loan.

Between 1828 and 1900, 238,000 assisted & 347,000 unassisted immigrants travelled to Australia. For a period in the mid-1840s severe drought and an economic depression caused assisted immigration to be suspended.

In 1851 with the discovery of gold in NSW and Victoria, immigrant ships brought thousands of people eager to make their fortunes at the diggings.

The sailing time from England was reduced to 80 days and the passengers often endured appalling conditions under unscrupulous shipowners. While people migrated from all over the world during the gold rush, most came from Scotland and England, followed by a large number of Chinese prospectors. Most of these immigrants were unassisted. Searching for Chinese ancestors may be difficult. Newspaper reports and government lists of miners' licenses may yield more information.

A gap in assisted immigration of 2-3 years from 1861 occurred due to government financial problems. Searching in Assisted Passenger lists will find few results in this period.

By 1869, there were six colonies in Australia – New South Wales, Tasmania, Western Australia, South Australia, Victoria and Queensland – all settled by British people. These separate colonies all had their own governors, parliaments and systems of government reporting to Britain.

Lists of the Scottish immigrants who came under the The Highlands and Islands Emigration Society scheme are available on *the Scottish Archive Network* at *http://www.scan.org.uk*

This resource has a great deal of background information on the Distressed Districts of Scotland and the work of the Society, including the emigration rules.

Sydney Cove, N.S.W. Emigrants Leaving the Ship
by O.W. Brierly, 1853   Mitchell Library, State Library of NSW

WHAT WAS IT LIKE TO BE A 19TH CENTURY IMMIGRANT?

Two systems of assisted immigration to New South Wales operated at various times throughout the 1800; the Bounty system, which was controlled in the colonies and involved the payment of part of the cost of passage by the Government to settlers who organised agents to select and send emigrants, usually from the United Kingdom, to the colonies and the Government system, which also assisted with the cost of passage and worked under regulations determined by colonial needs, but was administered in England. The Government system operated until 1840, and the Bounty system until 1845; and their costs were defrayed from funds raised by the sale of waste Crown land in the colony and by parishes and workhouses in the United Kingdom.

The two systems operated unchanged until the establishment of the Immigration Office and the appointment of the first Immigration Agent in Sydney, James Pinnock, in 1838. The Immigration Agent in Sydney was responsible for supervising shipping arrangements, and ensuring proper provision was made for the safety, comfort, and health of passengers during their voyage. The Agent provided information to emigrants, private individuals, institutions and parishes about the facilities existing for assisted emigration to New South Wales. He also attempted to prevent frauds being practiced on "the poorer class of emigrants who had been unscrupulously exploited by many of the shipowners". Pinnock was a strong supporter of the Bounty system . He was replaced as Immigration Agent by Francis Merewether from 1 August 1841 after he was accused by the Land and Emigration Commission of making "false statements intended to foster the bounty system in which 'large pecuniary interests are involved'".

In 1847, the second Bounty system of immigration was set up. The Colonial Land and Emigration Commissioners were entrusted with the selection and conveyance of migrants. On arrival in Sydney, the Immigration Board in Sydney decided whether or not shipping companies were entitled to payment for immigrants brought to the Colony. The Immigration Board was instituted to ensure that immigrants chosen for Bounty funding had the skills required in the colony and were of good character. There are a number of records in the Colonial Secretaries correspondence (NSW Archives) that tell of the Board's refusal to pay the Bounty to the Agent or the shipping company for a particular immigrant who was deemed unsuitable after misbehaviour during the journey, and questions asked regarding the possibility that some immigrants, or an Agent, had given false information regarding the skills and experience of an individual.

After 1852, most immigrants who received assisted passages did so through relatives and friends. For a short period after 1859, shipowners bore the costs of conveyance and were remunerated by the Board, and the small amount of government assistance that was provided was allotted by Legislative vote. In 1861, the Immigration Office was abolished and unassisted immigration which had been growing apace over the previous 10 years came into its own. People were, however, still receiving assisted passages in 1896. Under an administrative arrangement of 4 December 1896, the Chief Secretary was charged with business connected with immigration and the position of Immigration Agent appears to have been abolished.

THE SHIPS

The ships that brought settlers to Australia in the early 1800s were wooden ships with square sterns. They could carry about 290 passengers. They sailed badly and bobbed about like corks on the ocean. If well maintained they were safe, but they were often leaky and fire was a constant hazard. Bounty emigrants who travelled steerage had to put up with damp, dark and smelly, overcrowded quarters which encouraged the spread of pests and diseases. During the Gold Rush, in the 1850s, faster, sleek clipper ships were introduced. They were able to take up to more than 700 passengers and cut the travelling time to almost half by taking the shorter, but rougher Great Circle route, across the Southern Ocean and through the roaring 40s. While these vessels were larger and more comfortable, passengers often experienced petrifying, rough passages. Gradually ships became much larger and sailing times shorter as wooden sailing ships were replaced by iron vessels with steam engines.

The Journey

Guides to the voyage were provided to emigrants. Passengers had to provide enough clothing, utensils, and bedding for the long sea voyage, and even passengers who could afford their own cabin were required to equip it for the voyage. According to the Guide, a man should pack six shirts, three Guernsey or flannel shirts, six pairs of stockings, one pair of good stout shoes, one pair of good stout boots, one suit of warm outer clothing, one suit of light clothing and an extra pair of trousers, one light cap, and one warm cap, or southwester.

An adult woman should pack six chemises, six pairs of stockings, two flannel petticoats, two lighter petticoats, two pairs of good boots or shoes, one good warm cloak with hood, one hat or light bonnet for warm weather. A canvas bag held the clothing and supplies needed during the voyage. Everything else was packed into trunks and stowed in the ship's hold. Depending on the ship, and the weather, passengers could access their trunks only once or twice during a voyage. In bad conditions, many emigrants were stuck in damp, dirty clothes and bedding for weeks at a time.

Before boarding, passengers were divided into groups of between six and ten adults called 'messes'. Each mess would cook, eat and draw their rations together. Different classes of ticket dictated passengers' rations. Those who could afford it would often bring extra biscuits, jam, sugar, eggs, cheese and ham. Other than those in First Class cabins, passengers were required to cook their own food. Meals could include rice pudding, pea soup, oatmeal porridge and Sea Pie, a dish made on sailing vessels before canning or refrigeration were invented. It contained salted meat or fish, e.g. corned beef, with a crust made from flour and water. Passengers often experienced difficulties cooking and eating during storms at sea, when a strong roll or high swell could throw everything off the table.

Only one in ten emigrants could afford the price of a cabin. For the remaining passengers, both assisted and unassisted, home at sea was below the main deck in steerage quarters converted from cargo spaces.

This area was dark, crowded and close to the water line – when seas were rough passengers were often shut in with poor ventilation. There were berths lining the walls and a long dining table in the middle.

Passengers were usually given berths close to friends or passengers from the same region.

Steerage passengers were separated. Single men were usually housed in the bow (the front of the ship) and married couples and their children in the middle.

Single women were housed in the stern, closely supervised by a matron responsible for their physical and moral wellbeing. They were kept physically separated, usually fenced off, from the rest of the passengers and sometimes locked down at night.

Government regulations determined the daily routine on board British emigrant ships, as well as many private ships leaving English ports. Steerage passengers were required to clean their own berths, as were some second and third class passengers. The daily routine in steerage began at 6am with washing, dressing and tidying up before breakfast. Emigrants would then clear away and begin their chores: cleaning berths, scrubbing decks, and doing washing. Single men were expected to help out with extra tasks but for steerage passengers with children the days were long and hard. Tea was about 5pm, with lights out at 10pm. Between meals and housekeeping, steerage passengers used their leisure time to relax, play deck games and sports, read, sew, and write letters or journals. Timing of religious services and weekly inspections by the Surgeon Superintendent, wash days and daily cleaning of the 'coppers' were also regulated. Many ships had committees to help organise entertainments such as dances, theatrical or musical performances, and activities such as the publishing of ship newspapers.

Numerous journals, diaries and letters written by passengers on emigrant ships have been preserved in various state libraries, museums and maritime museums around Australia. A search of 'immigrant ships in the 1800s' will find the various collections.

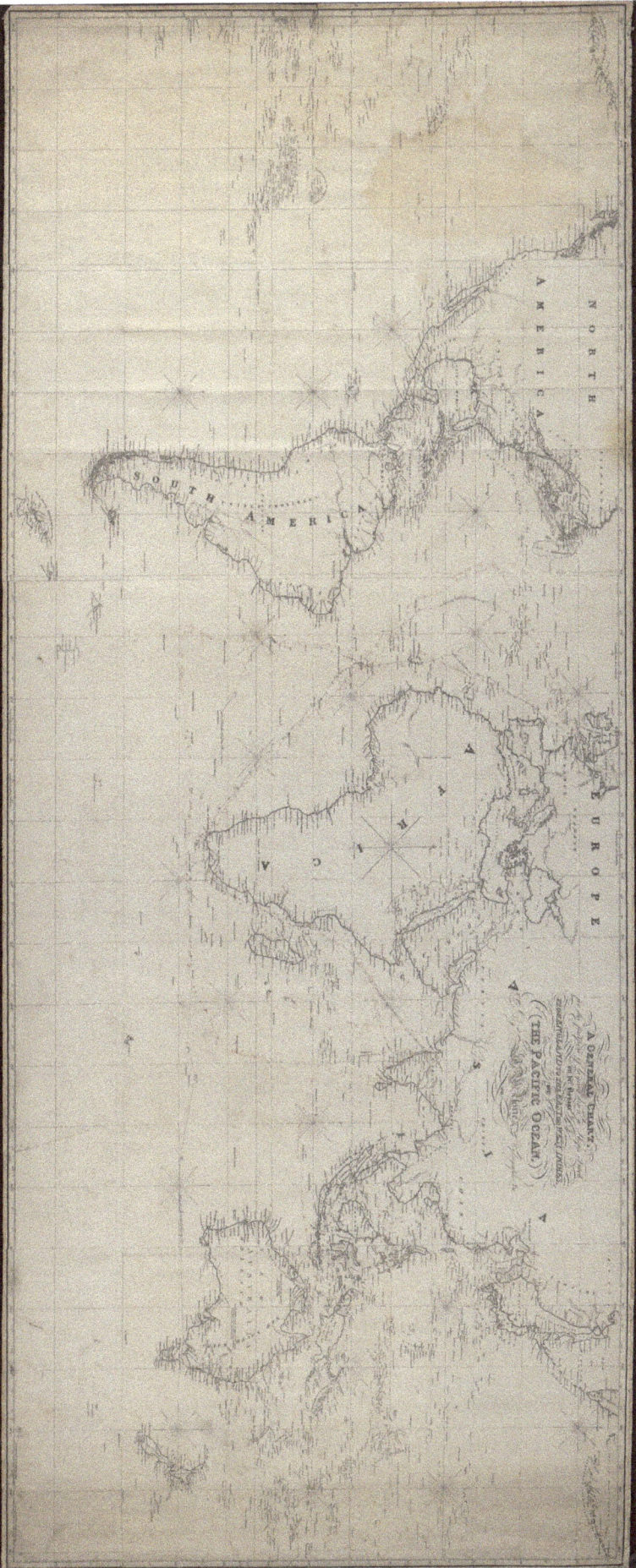

Norie, J. W. (1844). A general chart for the purpose of laying down a ship's track on her voyage from England to the East or West Indies or the Pacific Ocean Retrieved April 19, 2019, from http://nla.gov.au/nla.obj-231471221

A CASE STUDY IN IMMIGRATION- CATHERINE BROGAN

Ann Rebecca Collins was born in Campbelltown in 1845. Having firmly established her as the ancestor of Robert Sutton, I found her father's name, Edmund Collins, and that of her mother, Catherine Collins, on Ann's baptismal certificate. There was a further reference to Catherine on her son George's Baptismal Certificate from 1852, that gave her name as Catherine **Broaden** Collins

Although unable to find any record of either parent in the NSW Births or Baptisms, I found a marriage at the NSW Registry Office between Edmund Collins and Catherine **Brogan** in the church records for St Francis Xavier's Church in Wollongong on 15th August 1843. In 1983, Church records had not been digitised, so it meant a personal contact with the parish to see if they had a register. A kind parish secretary sent me a brief transcript of the marriage, just a simple record of the marriage and the witnesses. But at least I now had Catherine's maiden name, Brogan. Brogan and Broaden were near enough in pronunciation to allow a best guess that this was the same person.

A search of birth records for Catherine brought no results. With no birth records in Australia it was a natural progression to ask "If there are no birth records, might she have been born outside Australia?" My next step, therefore, was to go to State Archives office and search the microfiche immigration records pre-1843. I had no luck until 30 years later, when digitised records were available. My first search was in the Assisted Immigrants index in the NSW Records site, *https://www.records.nsw.gov. au/*. (To do this, select the Immigration and Shipping records. On this page is a very good guide to the records and then a list of the records available online.)

I chose the Assisted Immigrants Index and searched. The result was not good. All of the Catherine Brogans listed arrived after 1843, and therefore could not be our Catherine.

There was advice in the *Guide to the Index* that some records were not indexed and that, by following a link to Family Search, (https://www.familysearch.org/search/collection/1542665) a search of *Australia, New South Wales, Index to Bounty Immigrants, 1828-1842* on that site might prove useful for very early assisted immigrants. I clicked the link, entered Catherine's name, and bingo! There she was.

Selecting Catherine's name took me to the original index image, a photograph of the index card from the Archives. This gave me details of Catherine's name, age, occupation, religion and literacy, as well as her parents' names and the ship she arrived on.

Ship's records have even more details. I returned to the NSW Archives site and the Shipping Records. Now that I knew the ship and its arrival date, I could find it in the Index to Vessels Arrived 1837-1925. The Nabob's Record contained a digitised copy of the passenger list.

Index to Vessels Arrived, 1837 - 1925

Vessel name	Arrival Year
Nabob	1842

Arrival Month

Feb

Catherine Brogan was listed. I was able to view her detailed record as a single female immigrant on the Nabob. It gave further details of the agent who brought her out, her parents' names and the Bounty paid. Catherine's record gives her native place as Killeshandra, rather than Galway as it was on the index. It shows her as illiterate, which also varies from the Bounty Immigrant record.

UNMARRIED FEMALE IMMIGRANT

Name *Catherine Brogan*

Arrived by the Ship *Nabob*

Brought out by *A B Smith & Co*

Under protection of *John Crawford*

A native of *Gillerhandre*

Parents' Names *John & Mary Ewing*

Calling *House H*

Age *~~25~~ 24*

State, of bodily health, strength, and probable usefulness *V. Good*

Religion *Protestant*

Read or Write *neither*

Any complaints *none*

Remarks

Some years later, I found the Bounty Agent's report on Catherine, and a search brought to light a mention of her name in the enquiries of the Immigration Board into the suitability of some of the Nabob's Assisted Immigrants, in particular the behaviour of the single females. He reported;

"I was informed that the second mate was in the hospital with Elizabeth Mitchell (21 single), Catherine Brogan was watching at the door. On going down I saw Elizabeth but not the Second mate, who had hid himself. The circumstances looked suspicious."

I suspect Catherine had spirit and a good deal of cheek.

Further searching has come to a brick wall, as many records in Ireland were destroyed by fire and others remain undigitised. I cannot find her parents' records, nor a birth record for Catherine.

IMMIGRATION RESOURCES AND REFERENCES

Immigration records can be found in the following repositories;

- ∞ NSW State Records, https://www.records.nsw.gov.au
    - ∞ Indexes available online for immigrants to Sydney, Port Phillip, Moreton Bay and Newcastle
    - ∞ Immigration Agents' Lists & Immigration Board's Lists (search both).
    - ∞ Images of some passenger lists
    - ∞ Immigration deposit journals, 1853-65, 1875-1900
    - ∞ Reports by the Immigration Board on complaints of immigrants about their passage, 1838-87
    - ∞ Reports by the Immigration Agent on condition of immigrants and ships on their arrival, 1837-95
- ∞ Victoria Public Records Office http://www.prov.vic.gov.au
    - ∞ Unassisted overseas passengers 1852-1923
    - ∞ Assisted passengers 1839-1871
    - ∞ Government sponsored immigration was phased out in the 1870s and stopped altogether by 1883. Assisted passengers after 1871 are listed in Inwards Overseas Passenger Lists
- ∞ South Australia http://www.slsa.sa.gov.au/fh/passenger lists/BoundforSouthAustralia.htm
    - ∞ Ships to SA 1836 to 1851 Lists ships by year – however, there is no global name search. Includes inter-colonial and overseas arrivals
- ∞ Queensland http://www.archives.qld.gov.au/research/indexes.asp
    - ∞ QLD State Archives indexes
    - ∞ Assisted Immigration 1848-1912
    - ∞ Various other states records.
- ∞ Mariners and Ships in Australian waters http://www.mariners.records.nsw.gov.au/
- ∞ Ozships (Convictions) http://www.blaxland.com/ozships/
- ∞ "Australia Immigration Records Search - Public Immigration Records." Accessed December 7, 2018. http://australiapublicrecord.com/immigration-records/.
- ∞ Copeland, Ann. "Research Guides: Researching Your Ancestors from Great Britain and Ireland: Immigration Records - 1924 Onwards." Accessed December 7, 2018. https://guides.slv.vic.gov.au/britishislesancestors/immigration/1924on.
- ∞ Jen Willets. "Free Settler or Felon? Find Your Hunter Valley Ancestor." Accessed December 7, 2018. https://www.jenwilletts.com/index.htm.
- ∞ Johnson, Elspeth. "The Role of Family and Community in the Decision to Emigrate: Evidence from a Case Study of Scottish Emigration to Queensland 1885-88." Family and Community History, 2006. https://doi.org/http://dx.doi.org/10.1179/175138106X130059.
- ∞ Killick, John. "Transatlantic Steerage Fares, British and Irish Migration, and Return Migration, 1815-60." Economic History Review, 2014. https://doi.org/10.1111/1468-0289.12014.

ఴ National Archives of Australia. "Making Australia Home – National Archives of Australia, Australian Government." Accessed December 7, 2018. http://www.naa.gov.au/collection/explore/migration/home.aspx.

ఴ National Archives of Australia. "Passengers Arrivals Index | RecordSearch | National Archives of Australia." Accessed December 6, 2018. https://recordsearch.naa.gov.au/SearchNRetrieve/Interface/SearchScreens/PassengerSearch.aspx.

ఴ National Committee of Australia. "Australian Memory of the World | Imagine a World without Memories." Accessed December 6, 2018. http://www.amw.org.au/.

ఴ National Library of Australia. "Australian Shipping and Passenger Records | National Library of Australia." Accessed December 6, 2018. https://www.nla.gov.au/research-guides/finding-ship-and-passenger-records.

ఴ Num, Cora. "CoraWeb - Shipping and Migration." Accessed December 6, 2018. http://www.coraweb.com.au/categories/shipping-and-migration.

ఴ Huntsman, Leone. "Bounty Emigrants to Australia." Clogher Record 17, no. 3 (2002): 801-12. doi:10.2307/27699475.

ఴ https://www.nma.gov.au/audio/audio/not-just-ned-irish-in-australia-series/transcripts/irish-immigrants-from-austral

ఴ http://www.maritimetas.org/collection-displays/displays/over-seas-stories-tasmanian-migrants/journey-sailing-ship

ఴ https://www.sl.nsw.gov.au/stories/shipboard-19th-century-emigrant-experience. "Shipboard" is a collection of the State Library of NSW that delivers an insight into the immigrant experience of the second half of the 19th Century, including sketches made on board by passengers, exceprts from letters and diaries and paintings.

ఴ Norie, J. W. (1844). A general chart for the purpose of laying down a ship's track on her voyage from England to the East or West Indies or the Pacific Ocean Retrieved April 19, 2019, from http://nla.gov.au/nla.obj-231471221

ADD YOUR OWN REFERENCES HERE

"The Australian and New Zealand troops have indeed proved themselves worthy sons of the Empire."

GEORGE R.I.

MILITARY ANCESTORS

When we come across an Australian or British ancestor who was a soldier, airman or sailor, we often want to find out about their military career, particularly if he/she was involved in a notable military campaign, or if family legend has given them hero status.

- ෨ When did they enlist?
- ෨ How old were they when they enlisted?
- ෨ Were they married or single?
- ෨ In what unit did they serve? Did they stay in that unit for the whole war?
- ෨ When did they leave Australia/Britain?
- ෨ Where did they go?
- ෨ What battles did they fight in?
- ෨ Did they get wounded or sick?
- ෨ Were they promoted?
- ෨ Did they receive any awards/honours?
- ෨ Did they commit any offences?
- ෨ Did they die in overseas, and if so where were they buried?
- ෨ When did they return to Australia?
- ෨ How did the war affect them? What did they do after the war, and
- ෨ Were they memorialized in any way overseas or at home?

These are mainly factual questions that can generally be answered by consulting online research services such as Ancestry.com, Fold3 or Forces War Records, which contain records from relevant institutions.

However, it is always wise to consult the records of the original institutions where possible. You may find some records that are not available on the subscription sites, for example, the military records of Scotland start in the 17th century, the Australian Nominal Rolls held by the Australian Archives are invaluable.

Military records are the official records of a country's defence forces. Depending on the country, they may include the records of army, navy, air force, coastguard, marines, militia, etc. They usually contain documents that record;

- ෨ a person's service over time,
- ෨ any training they undertook,
- ෨ medals or promotions they received,
- ෨ any active service in a war zone,
- ෨ any injuries or misdemeanours
- ෨ their post-service pension.

Many family members may have served in the armed forces. They may have enlisted for a single conflict, e.g. World War I, or made the defence force their career. Military and naval records can reveal many useful genealogical facts that could be missing from the usual vital records repositories. It may be difficult to find civil records of people who served in the armed forces, as they may rarely have been at home. If so, they won't be found in any census returns, birth, marriage or death events that happened while on service.

SEARCHING MILITARY RECORDS ON ANCESTRY.COM

Before you attempt a search for your ancestor's military records, find as much information as you can. Talk to the family and ascertain whether he/she had any medals or honours. Think about the old war stories that were told by grandparents, they may have referred to the service to which they belonged. Look for old log books, diaries or letters. What you are seeking is a person's service number, reference to a regiment or unit or the type of service medal they might have been awarded.

Photographs of the person in uniform are invaluable as they usually have the insignia of the service, regiment or unit on badges or flashes. Once you have gathered as much as you can, then go to the records.

The most proficient search for an ancestor's military records is through Ancestry.com.au. If you do not have a subscription, make the time to go to the local library and use their library edition.

Fill in the search screen with the information you have. If all you have is the name and date of birth, that's okay, it only means you will receive more results that are not relevant.

Once you have a list of records, you'll see that at the top of the list are the most likely matches. There are two Robert Andrew Mayors on this list, but one is in the USA and World War II. This search is for Robert Andrew Mayor who fought in the British Army in World War I.

Clicking on his name takes me to the details of this record.

If the original document or index entry is available, clicking "**View**" will allow me to see it, and to save it to my computer or email it to myself.

All Military results for Robert Andrew Mayor

The first page you see may not be the last. You may find that there are many pages in the record, so make sure you save each one. You will find so much detailed information in each page.

Make sure to save all of the pages in the record. They may require saving each page individually, however,the initial save at the beginning of the record may result in all pages being saved in one PDF document. Check first by saving the initial page. Open the saved document in Acrobat Reader and see how many pages there are. If there is more than one, you probably have the entire record from that dataset.

Robert Andrew Mayor's military record.

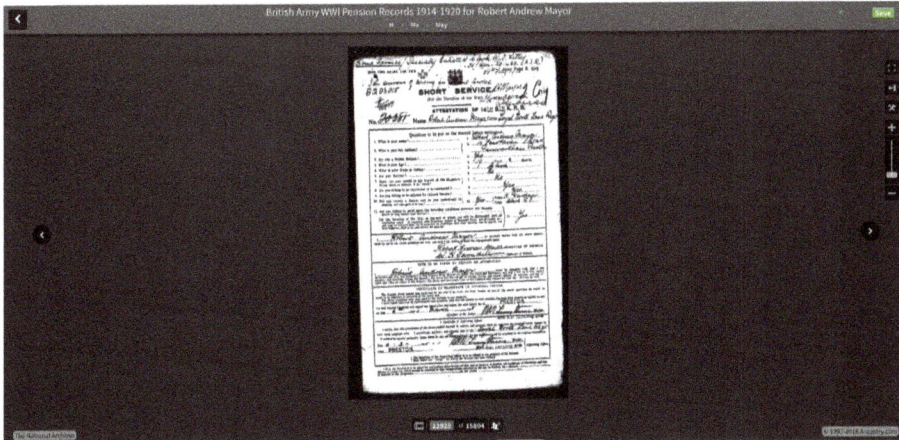

Robert Andrew Mayor
in the British Army WWI Pension Records 1914-1920

Name:	Robert Andrew Mayor
Gender:	Male
Birth Date:	abt 1896
Age:	19
Document Year:	1915
Residence Place:	10 Fairhaven Road, Penwortham Priston
Regimental Number:	20381
Regiment Name:	Loyal North Lancashire Regiment
Form Title:	Short Service Attestation
Number of Images:	22
Other Records:	Search for 'Robert Andrew Mayor' in other WWI collections

Family Members:	Name	Relation to Soldier
	Robert Andrew Mayor	Self (Head)
	Mary Mayor	Mother

Send Your Find Home!

Enter your email address and we will send you a link to your personalized Discovery Page where you can view and download all of the great finds you make while here.

Send document

We value your privacy. *Read our Privacy Statement*

🖶 *View printer-friendly*

HOW TO THE FIND INFORMATION YOU SEEK.

Look through the pages to find the *Attestation*. If it is a British record it will look like the one on the opposite page.

Note that there is evidence of damage on the document.

Examine the record for Richard Ambler.

Work through the document from the top.

'Short Service' means that the soldier has signed up for the duration of the war with the colours (the army) and the army reserve.

The soldiers service number, name and corps are listed.

Notice that Richard has a "**P**" in front of his number - "P/3492". He is assigned to the military foot police. (In civilian life, Richard was a policeman. His father,also Richard, had been part of the British constabulary in Ireland. Richard was born in 1891 in Birr, Ireland.)

A series of questions and answers follows, including;

- ∞ his address,
- ∞ age,
- ∞ trade/calling and
- ∞ marital status.

This was the first inkling I had that Richard was married. Further on in the record, on the following page, I was able to find his wife's and child's name. There is his signature, which can be valuable if a later date you need to distinguish him from others of the same name on such documents as wills, probate documents, contracts, deeds etc.

Following are the date and place of enlistment.

Richard enlisted in the military foot police on 17th November 1916 but the records also has an approval date of July, 1916.

Always check the written notes on the attestation.

In Richard's case, the only note is that this was a Certified True Copy of his attestation and not the original.

Other Attestations have had notes as to transfer from one Regiment or Unit to another, and notes of battle service or honours and pensions received.

On the second page of the nine pages of his record, Richard's physical description and the names and ages of his wife and child are recorded.

THE BURNT DOCUMENTS

By the end of the war in 1918, more than seven million men and women had seen service in the British army.

Unfortunately, more than half of their service records were destroyed in September 1940, when a German bombing raid struck the War Office repository in Arnside Street, London.

However, an estimated 2.8 million service records survived the bombing or were reconstructed from the records of the Ministry of Pensions. This means that there is a roughly 40% chance of finding the service record of a soldier who was discharged at some time between 1914 and 1920. These are called "The Burnt Documents".

The Burnt Documents are only available to the public on microfilm due to the amount of damage from fire and water. They are too delicate to be handled.

Some of the documents have been digitised from the microfilm and more are coming online all the time.

The Attestation opposite is part of this set of records. The British records are fiddly to search, but the effort is well worth it.

Personal details

Trade or calling

Previous service

Called up?

Terms of Service

Particulars of marriage give you the maiden name, marriage date and address, which helps in further searching.

Military History gives you dates of service and sometimes the campaign histories. This one is very sparse.

AUSTRALIAN MILITARY RECORDS

Like any organisation, a military body needs to know who its members are in order to track such things as experience, training, pay, progress through the ranks, names of any dependents a member might have in case a pension needs to be paid, information on the next of kin in case of death and so on. The defence force bureaucracy creates a vast number of different types of records in order to track its members. For this, as family historians, we can be thankful.

Often, the first record created is an attestation record. These are the forms that are created when someone signs up for military service. They contain a varying amount of information but you will usually find, names, birth information, names of the next of kin and addresses.

Other records you might find will depend on the ancestor's branch of service, how long they served, if they served overseas, whether they got into trouble, and whether they were wounded or died. The military also created birth, marriage and death records recording any that happened on a military base or through the auspices of a military chaplain or other officiate.

In searching military records, your success in finding information will depend in part on:

∾ Whether they were an officer vs. enlisted person, as generally it is easier to track officers as more records were kept about them and

∾ Whether you know their service number, regiment's name, the ship served on and so on.

ORGANISATION AND REPOSITORIES OF RECORDS

Many record sets are not arranged by individuals' name.

If you are looking at a resource that has not been indexed, you may have to resort to looking page by page through the resource for your ancestor. Members of your family may help you, however, many databases that include individuals' records are searchable by name.

In Australia, the major institutions that hold defence force records are;

∾ The National Archives of Australia

∾ The Australian War Memorial and

∾ The Commonwealth War Graves Commission.

∾ If your Australian ancestor was killed or wounded overseas while fighting with combined forces, there may be records in the UK or Europe.

∾ If they were killed in wartime and buried overseas, the *Commonwealth War Graves Commission* is the source of information to go to.

While many military records have been digitized and indexed online, there are many more that are only available in physical archives. Living in Australia makes this a difficult and expensive task. However, it's an area that is developing rapidly so keep checking to see if what you are seeking has recently been made available online.

By exploring those institutions and consulting the records they hold, you will probably find answers to many of your questions. Unfortunately Ancestry.com.au requires a subscription to Fold3 to see original documents. A result similar to this one is the best you can do to retrieve information without the Fold3 subscription.

The Australian National Archives hold military records for Australian personnel from the founding of the Australian Army through to modern conflicts. Not all are digitised.

A search will give you the details of the records, however, unless someone has previously requested the record, it will not have been digitised and cannot be viewed electronically unless a fee is paid. If you are the first person to request a record, you will need to pay the fee and apply to be sent a link to the downloadable PDF file. The next person to request it will then be able to view the record online.

The Australian War Memorial has a database of records and photographs that is searchable online. The research assistants at the AWM are most helpful and a phone call or a visit to Canberra are well worth the effort. The also hold objects such as diaries, both personal and unit or war diaries, medals, honours etc that can be viewed.

The digitized newspaper database on Trove can be searched for lists of casualties during wartime, troop and unit movements and news from battle grounds. The records held by those publications are less helpful in answering other questions:

- Why did your soldier enlist?
- How did he feel about fighting?
- How he did he feel about seeing a mate killed or wounded?
- How did he feel about killing another human being?
- How did he feel about being wounded or sick?
- What did he eat?
- How did he relax when he was off duty?

Answers to these questions can only be found in letters, diaries or memoirs. Unfortunately, soldiers did not always write their true feelings in letters and cards. They often put a brave face on things so as not to be seen as weak, or to not worry family, particularly mothers and sisters.

Try searching in the letters, diaries and personal documents sections of Trove to get a better understanding of what soldiers told their family in letters and how that might differ from their diaries.

Military records can reveal much about a soldier's life and movements. To tell their story and understand the decisions they made and the actions they took means delving into as many sources of information as you can find.

Regimental diaries, airmens' logs and ships' logs, while they may not mention your ancestor by name, give a graphic picture of what was happening around him/her in the trenches, in the air or on the sea.

CASE STUDY - ROBERT ANDREW MAYOR, BRITISH ARMY WWI.

Home Service / Specially Enlisted Clerk. W.O. Letter 35/Gen./No 1230. (A.I.R.)

25th Feby 1915

(2918b) W 8321 Sub 1252 11/14 J F W 27

Gen. No. 2325

Army Form B. 2505.

B 203015

R/46901.

I am desirous of serving for General Service R A Mayor

SHORT SERVICE.

(For the Duration of the War). Shageboook Con 14th Bn KRR

ATTESTATION OF 14TH BTN K.R.R.

No. 20381 Name Robert Andrew Mayor Corps Loyal North Lanc Regt

Questions to be put to the Recruit before enlistment.

1. What is your name?	1.	Robert Andrew Mayor
2. What is your full Address?	2.	10 Fairhaven Road Penwortham Preston
3. Are you a British Subject?	3.	Yes
4. What is your Age?	4.	19 Years 2 Months.
5. What is your Trade or Calling?	5.	Clerk
6. Are you Married?	6.	No
7. Have you ever served in any branch of His Majesty's Forces, naval or military, if so,* which?	7.	No
8. Are you willing to be vaccinated or re-vaccinated?	8.	Yes
9. Are you willing to be enlisted for General Service?	9.	Yes
10. Did you receive a Notice, and do you understand its meaning, and who gave it to you?	10. Yes	Name H. Gardner Corps Clerk R.O.
11. Are you willing to serve upon the following conditions provided His Majesty should so require your services?		
For the duration of the War, at the end of which you will be discharged with all convenient speed. If employed with Hospitals, depots of Mounted Units, and as Clerks, etc., you may be retained after the termination of hostilities until your services can be spared, but such retention shall in no case exceed six months.	11.	Yes

I, Robert Andrew Mayor do solemnly declare that the above answers made by me to the above questions are true, and that I am willing to fulfil the engagements made.

Robert Andrew Mayor SIGNATURE OF RECRUIT.

W. H. Farndell Signature of Witness.

OATH TO BE TAKEN BY RECRUIT ON ATTESTATION.

I, Robert Andrew Mayor swear by Almighty God, that I will be faithful and bear true Allegiance to His Majesty King George the Fifth, His Heirs and Successors, and that I will, as in duty bound, honestly and faithfully defend His Majesty, His Heirs and Successors, in Person, Crown, and dignity against all enemies, and will observe and obey all orders of His Majesty, His Heirs and Successors, and of the Generals and Officers set over me. So help me God.

CERTIFICATE OF MAGISTRATE OR ATTESTING OFFICER.

The Recruit above named was cautioned by me that if he made any false answer to any of the above questions he would be liable to be punished as provided in the Army Act.

The above questions were then read to the Recruit in my presence.

I have taken care that he understands each question, and that his answer to each question has been duly entered as replied to, and the said Recruit has made and signed the declaration and taken the oath before me at PRESTON.

on this 6 day of March 1915

Signature of the Justice .... Major, 30th R.D. Recruiting Area.

† Certificate of Approving Officer.

I certify that this Attestation of the above-named Recruit is correct, and properly filled up, and that the required forms appear to have been complied with. I accordingly approve, and appoint him to the ‡ Loyal North Lanc Regt

If enlisted by special authority, Army Form B. 203 (or other authority for the enlistment) will be attached to the original attestation.

Date 6 - 3 - 1915

Place PRESTON.

.... Major, 30th R.D. Recruiting Area. Approving Officer.

† The signature of the Approving Officer is to be affixed in the presence of the Recruit.
‡ Here insert the "Corps" for which the Recruit has been enlisted.

* If so, the Recruit is to be asked the particulars of his former service, and to produce, if possible, his Certificate of Discharge and Certificate of Character, which should be returned to him conspicuously endorsed in red ink, as follows, viz.—(Name) ____ re-enlisted in the (Regiment) ____ on the (Date) ____

THE FOLLOWING IS THE RESULT OF THE SEARCH FOR ROBBIE MAYOR, DEMONSTRATING A TRAIL OF MILITARY RECORDS THAT SOLVED A FAMILY MYSTERY, ONLY TO REVEAL A FURTHER BRICK WALL.

Robert Andrew Mayor was my paternal Great Uncle. Born in 1896 in Penwortham, England, I knew he had fought in WWI and that he had returned a changed man, emigrating to the USA in 1919. His four sisters were told by their father that Robbie had died in a gangland shooting in Chicago, USA, in 1920 at the height of the Prohibition.. He had been with a gang, bootlegging alcohol between Canada and the USA and had been found, shot, in his boarding house room. Robbie's story intrigued me. It was in 2014, the centenary year of the start of World War I that I chose him as the subject of my first Mayor family history research project.

I already had Uncle Robbie's birth record, listing his birth date and parents, and a census record with the family's address. I knew he had been a clerk in a printing factory. I commenced my research with the British military records. To access these I needed to go through Ancestry.com, as the only other way to search the archives is in person. My search brought up a number of documents;

- ➷ Robbie's attestation and enlistment documents
- ➷ His service record (regiment, company, overseas service)

His medical records

- ➷ His pension records.

Examine the attestation document opposite. There is an incredible amount of information on this form.

1. Robert Andrew Mayor's full name, address, age, occupation and marital status. This enabled me to confirm the matches with records I already had and be sure that this was indeed my Great Uncle Robbie.
2. His signature. This enabled me later on to validate other documents.
3. The conditions under which he <u>first</u> enlisted and the regiment he enlisted in. This document indicates he was re-enlisting in the army to serve in a different way.

The handwritten notes around the top of the form tell this last story.

Underlined are the words "Home Service/ Specially enlisted Clerk. W.S. Letter 35 Kew/HS1430 (A.I.R.) 25th July 1915."

Robbie was not meant to be serving overseas. He had originally enlisted in the Loyal North Lancashire Regiment to work as a clerk in England. However, this is an Attestation Form that has the stamp of the 14th Battalion of the K.R.R. - the Kings Royal Rifles - a fighting unit of the British Army.

Written on the form in pencil is "I am desirous of serving for general[?] service" and is signed R.A. Mayor. It would seem that, although he had enlisted for Home Service, the vigorous recruitment campaign mounted in his home town of Preston that year, by Lord Derby, had the desired effect and Robbie decided to go to the front.

According to his military and medical records, Robert Andrew Mayor was a rifleman in the Second Company of the 14th Brigade of the King's Royal Rifles. He arrived in Belgium in 1916 and fought on the Somme.

From Regimental Diaries, accessed through Ancestry.com, I gained a picture of what life was like for riflemen at the time he was there; of numbers of casualties and living conditions.

Robbie's medical records show that, as a result of the horrors he experienced in battle, he was severely shell-shocked. He suffered from epilepsy, seizures and incontinence. He spent time in hospital in France and England and was discharged from the army as unfit for further service due to 'shell-shock' in 1917.

The Preston newspapers of 1913-1919 contain accounts of the recruitment campaign, editorials and news reports recorded during the war and letters to the editor from concerned townsfolk between the start of WWI and 1918.

Many of them expressed negative attitudes towards soldiers who were brought home from the battlefields and discharged early due to what we now know as Post Traumatic Stress Disorder, then called 'shell-shock'. These men were regarded by many as cowards and malingerers and rejected by much of the population. Robbie's records show that, following his discharge, he was packed off to Glasgow to work in the shipyards as a riveter and consequently suffered the loss of an eye in a workplace accident. It took until 1919 for him to receive his pension.

There is more to Robbie's story. Searches of the immigration records revealed an application for US Citizenship made by Robert Andrew Mayor in July 1925. The personal details and his physical description of having lost an eye matched those of Uncle Robbie. I compared the signatures on his attestation form, his immigration documents and the application. They matched. Searches of social security and military records revealed a US Draft Registration Card, completed and signed by Robert Andrew Mayor in 1942, just after Pearl Harbour. Again, all details and the signature matched.

I firmly believe that Robert Andrew Mayor, my Great Uncle Robbie, did not die in 1920. He may have married. He may have descendants in the USA. The search continues.

 I will never know why my Great Grandfather told his family that Robbie was dead. I can only surmise that it was out of shame and a wish for his daughters not to contact their brother or to go looking for him. One thing is sure, without the immigration and military records of both the UK and the USA, we would never have known Robbie, the man. He would always have been the little Scottish Soldier in the only photograph we have of him.

Robert Andrew Mayor, Carte De Visite, C1900   Ambler-Sutton Collection   Chris Sutton 2018

MILITARY RESOURCES & REFERENCES

Resources

- Ancestry.com. "Fold3 - Historical Military Records." Accessed December 8, 2018. https://www.fold3.com/.
- Archives, The National. "How to Look for Records of... Second World War." Accessed December 8, 2018. http://www.nationalarchives.gov.uk/help-with-your-research/research-guides/second-world-war/.
- "How to Look for Records of...British Army Soldiers of the First World War." Accessed December 8, 2018. http://www.nationalarchives.gov.uk/help-with-your-research/research-guides/british-army-soldiers-after-1913/.
- Australian Defence Forces. "How to Research Family History | Australian Army." Accessed December 8, 2018. https://www.army.gov.au/our-history/how-to-research-family-history.
- Department of Culture, Heritage and the Gaeltacht. "Military And Police Records - Irish Genealogy." Accessed December 8, 2018. https://www.irishgenealogy.ie/en/irish-records-what-is-available/military-and-police-records.
- Government of Canada. "Personnel Records of the First World War - Library and Archives Canada." Accessed December 8, 2018. https://www.bac-lac.gc.ca/eng/discover/military-heritage/first-world-war/personnel-records/Pages/personnel-records.aspx.
- Imperial War Museum, UK. "Lives of the First World War." Accessed December 8, 2018. https://livesofthefirstworldwar.org.
- National Archives of Australia. "Army – World War II." Accessed December 8, 2018. http://www.naa.gov.au/collection/explore/defence/service-records/army-wwii.aspx.
- National Archives of Australia, Australian Government. "Army – World War I." Accessed December 8, 2018. http://www.naa.gov.au/collection/explore/defence/service-records/army-wwi.aspx.
- The Australian War Memorial. "Personal Service Records: Australian Service." Accessed December 8, 2018. https://www.awm.gov.au/research/guide/service-records.
- The U.S. National Archives and Records Administration. "Online Military Records in AAD | National Archives." Accessed December 8, 2018. https://www.archives.gov/research/military/veterans/aad.html.
- US Government. "Veterans Documents and Personnel Records | USAGov." Accessed December 8, 2018. https://www.usa.gov/veterans-documents.
- National Records of Scotland. "National Records of Scotland." National Records of Scotland. Accessed December 8, 2018. https://www.nrscotland.gov.uk/research/guides/military-records.

References

1. Ancestry 1911 England Census, Census Returns of England and Wales, 1911. Kew, Surrey, England: The National Archives of the UK (TNA), 1911. Data imaged from the National Archives, London, England.
2. Ancestry Border Crossings: From Canada to U.S., 1895-1956 Records of the Immigration and Naturalization Service, RG 85. Washington, D.C.: National Archives and Records Administration.
3. Ancestry British Army WWI Medal Rolls Index Cards, 1914-1920
4. Ancestry British Army WWI Pension Records 1914-1920 War Office: Soldiers' Documents from Pension Claims, First World War (Microfilm Copies); (The National Archives Microfilm Publication WO364
5. Ancestry Canadian Passenger Lists, 1865-1935 Passenger Lists, 1865–1935.
6. Ancestry.com.au; London, England, Church of England Births and Baptisms, 1813-1906
7. Ancestry Declarations of Intention for Citizenship, 1903 – 1981 National Archives at Chicago; Chicago, Illinois; ARC Title: Declarations of Intention for Citizenship, 1903 - 1981; NAI Number: 6756420;
8. Ancestry Detroit Border Crossings and Passenger and Crew Lists, 1905-1957 Detroit, Michigan. Card Manifests (Alphabetical) of Individuals Entering through the Port of Detroit, Michigan, 1906-1954.
9. Ancestry England & Wales, FreeBMD Birth Index, 1837-1915 General Register Office. England and Wales Civil Registration Indexes. London, England.
10. Ancestry New York Passenger Lists, 1820-1957 Passenger Lists of Vessels Arriving at New York, New York, 1820-1897; (National Archives Microfilm Publication M237, 675 rolls); Records of the U.S. Customs Service
11. Ancestry Passenger record Outward Passenger Lists, 1890-1960
12. Ancestry U.S. World War II Draft Registration Cards, 1942 United States, Selective Service System. Selective Service Registration Cards, World War II: Fourth Registration. National Archives and Records Administration Branch

13. Bayley, William A. History of Campbelltown: New South Wales Campbelltown N.S.W., Campbelltown Municipal Council, 1965.

14. British Library: British Newspaper Archive Online http://www.britishnewspaperarchive.co.uk

15. Forces War Records, Melksham, Wilts, https://www.forces-war-records.co.uk/units/1508/kings-royal-rifle-corps/ Accessed 28 April 2017

16. Jen Willets Free Settler or Felon? The Convict Ship Recovery, http://www.jenwilletts.com/convict_ship_recovery_1836.htm

17. Kings Royal Rifle Corps Association, London, England Online http://www.krrcassociation.com/index.php/history Accessed 4/5/2017

18. Long, Long Trail website http://www.longlongtrail.co.uk Accessed 2/5/2017

19. NSW Registrar of Birth Death & Marriage (NSWBDM)   Burial Certificate Parish of Sofala 1852 Number 1491 Vol:38 Edmund COLLINS

20. NSW Registrar of Birth Death & Marriage (NSWBDM) Baptism Certificate Parish Records of Sofala, county of Roxborough 1852 Number 2363 Vol:38 George COLLINS.

21. NSW Registrar of Birth Death & Marriage (NSWBDM) Baptism Certificate Parish Records of St Peter County of Cumberland 1846 Number 1563 Vol:31 Ann COLLINS.

22. NSW Registrar of Birth Death & Marriage (NSWBDM) Marriage Certificate Roman Catholic Church, Wollongong, 46/1843 V184346 123 Edmund COLLINS/Catherine BROGAN

23. NSW Registrar of Birth Death & Marriage (NSWBDM) Church of England, Campbelltown, Baptism, 20th May 1846,1563 Vol:31 Ann COLLINS

24. New South Wales and Tasmania, Australia, Convicts Applications to Marry, 1826 to 1851. Edmund COLLINS/ Catherine ROGAN

25. New South Wales, Australia Convict Ship Muster Rolls and Related Records, 1790-1849 Edmund COLLINS

26. NSW State Records: New South Wales, Australia, Convict Registers of Conditional and Absolute Pardons, 1788 -1870

27. NSW State Records: New South Wales, Australia, Pardons and Tickets of Leave, 1824 – 1867

28. NSW State Records: New South Wales, Australia, Convict Indents, 1788 -1842

29. Northampton County Council Prison and Reformatory Records, Northampton, Northamptonshire, England. http://www.northamptonshire.gov.uk/en/councilservices/Community/archives/Documents/PDF%20Documents/Prison%20and%20reformatory%20records.pdf

30. Peter Leese, 'Problems Returning Home: The British Psychological Casualties of the Great War', The Historical Journal, vol. 40, No. 4, 1997, pp. 1055–1067.

31. Preston Herald 1st January – 30th April 1915 British Newspaper Archive Online   http://www.britishnewspaperarchive.co.uk   Accessed 20th April 2017

32. Shell Shock and the Emotional History of the First World War. A lecture by Professor Jay Winter. British Academy 9 July 2014. YouTube. Duration 52:06 minutes.

ADD YOUR OWN REFERENCES HERE;

Understanding their Lives; Looking Outside the BDMs

IMAGES OF FAMILY

"Photography takes an instant out of time,
altering life by holding it still."

Dorothea Lange

In this section you will learn how to use photographs as clues in the search for information about your ancestors.

The principles of projecting an image through light, by having light come through a small hole into a darkened space, have been known since antiquity.

In the 18th century, more elaborate set-ups used mirrors to turn the projected image the right way up.

Dating photographs is a forensic process. There are steps that can be followed to come to an educated guess at the approximate date it was taken.

1. Take the person out of the photo. Ignore the people in the portrait and concentrate on what is around them.

2. Look at the corners, what is there? Often we forget to look at corners and miss clues as to where and when the photo may have been taken.

3. Look at the background. The background may tell you where the photo was taken if it isn't a studio portrait. Look for objects, equipment, machinery, road signs anything that provide information.

4. Look at the foreground in the same way.

5. Put the person back and examine clothing, objects, jewellery, etc. that they are wearing.

6. Now tell the story that has been revealed.

As an exercise, examine this photo and see how much information you can glean from it.

  ⁖ When do you think it was taken?

  ⁖ What was the environment?

  ⁖ What can you see that will give you a clue?

The answers to the mystery will be revealed.

DATING BY PHOTOGRAPHIC PROCESS

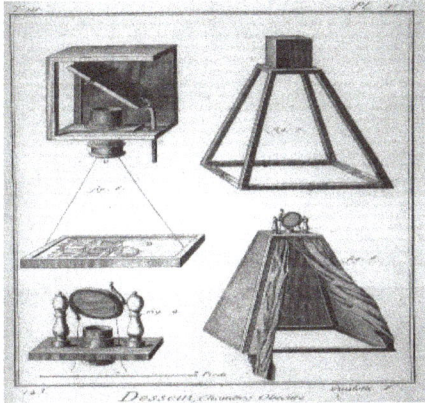

Portraits in the 19th Century were primarily confined to the studio. The studio gave photographers a controlled environment in which they could work. It allowed the photographer ease of set up. Cameras of the time were large and cumbersome. Materials were delicate and required careful handling and time-sensitive processing. The studio provided an aesthetically controlled space with props and backdrops on hand to support the stylistic expectations of portraiture.

Different processes evolved across the 19th Century. A clue as to the approximate date of a photograph can be gleaned from the type of process used in creating it.

DAGUERREOTYPE (1839)

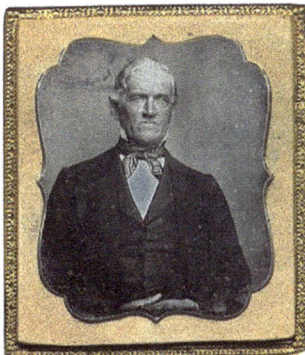

Daguerreotypes can be identified by their mirrored appearance. They can be seen as a positive or negative image, depending on the angle. They were made in a range of sizes and are usually found in small leather cases with hinged covers. However, they may also housed in glazed wooden frames. While daguerreotype were highly fashionable, they were still expensive, fragile and relatively rare.

CALOTYPE (1841)

The advantage to the Calotype process was that it could be used to make multiple prints. However, the images were not as sharp, detailed or stable as the daguerreotype. While Daguerre had shared his process in return for a stipend from the French government, Talbot patented his process. It was therefore not used very often.

AMBROTYPE (1851);

Ambrotypes captured an image on coated glass (based on the collodion wet plate process) that, when backed by a dark material, appeared as a positive image. This gives them their characteristic grey appearance.

TINTYPE (1853)

The tintype used the same process for capturing the image, but used lacquered iron rather than glass. Tintypes are often found in albums, small portraits many to the page. They are very rare. *If you find one, do not remove it from the mount or frame.* You will destroy its value.

PRINTING FROM GLASS NEGATIVES

The collodion process, which captures a negative image on treated glass, enabled the production of multiple prints of the same image. The common collodion wet plate process required photographers to work quickly under controlled conditions to prepare the glass and take the photograph before it dried. Nonetheless, this technical innovation propelled the increasing ubiquity of photography.

MODERN PAPER PRINTING METHODS

From the 1860s, the industrial manufacture of pre-sensitised photographic paper enabled the spread of photography.

From 1871, silver gelatin prints (also called developing out paper prints) rapidly became popular. Silver gelatin prints have multiple layers (substrate, baryta coating, gelatin) on paper or resin coated paper. Tones in the image are black, grey and white/cream/beige. Silver gelatin prints are still used today by some artists and enthusiasts.

A common sign of deterioration in photos created through this process is silver mirroring, where the silver becomes visible on the surface of the image. ***Do not try to remove this.***

USING PHOTOGRAPHIC SURROUNDS TO DATE PHOTOS.

PRE-1860s

Studio backgrounds are generally plain, with the subject seated.

1870s

More sophisticated backgrounds and props including columns, drapes and banisters. Furniture was usually heavily upholstered.

1880s

The rustic look was very popular. In addition to backdrops painted as spectacular landscapes, props could include rough wooden fences and gates, grasses and tree stumps.

1890s AND EARLY TWENTIETH CENTURY

Cane furniture and rugs were common elements.

DATING BY TYPE OF PHOTOGRAPH

CARTE DE VISITE (CDV)

Appeared: 1859

Peaked: 1863-1877

Waned: 1877-1882

The carte de visite changed consumer photography as much as the introduction of any other type of photograph. Previous photographs were unique, one-of-a-kind pictures, now the consumer could buy several copies of a picture, and share them with friends and relatives. Assembling a collection of family photographs became a popular tradition. Photograph albums began appearing in the early 1860s, starting a collecting activity that has lasted to the present time.

- ཨ Image on thin paper, mounted on card stock
- ཨ Early cards very thin, became thicker about 1870, and even more about 1880
- ཨ Most exhibit the classic sepia tone
- ཨ Card Thickness
  Card Corners - Pre-1870 corners are square
  Image Size on Card – Smaller is older
  Card Borders - Thin borders are pre-1868
- ཨ Studio Props & Background - Elaborate props/background is post-1870
- ཨ Dated CDV

CABINET CARD

The Cabinet Card was the most common family portrait.

Most cabinet cards are 6 ½"x 4 ¼"

Appeared: 1866

Peaked: 1875-1895

Waned: 1896-1900

Initially, cabinet cards were made from natural raw Bristol board, both front and back.

In the mid-1870s the backs were coated with soft off-white or even light pastel ink.

The two most advertised card colours were primrose (pale yellow) and pearl (rich off-white) though light pink, blue, and green can be found.

Dark cards were popular from 1885 to 1895.

DATING FROM FASHION

There are some general principles to bear in mind when attempting to date a photograph from the clothing worn.

- ❧ Start with the type of photo.
- ❧ Women's fashion changes more often than men's fashion.
- ❧ There are fewer portrait photographs of the poor and therefore you will find less examples of poor people's clothing.
- ❧ Australian fashion lagged behind Britain and America.
- ❧ Poor people often wore hand-me-downs and therefore the date could be earlier than the fashion suggests. Use general fashion history timelines to start the dating process but +/- 5 years.

For example, the photograph below was taken on the Australian goldfields during the late 1800s. There is a good variety of men's clothing styles here. By comparing your photograph with this one, you could look at collars, ties, lapel lengths, waistcoats and hats to find similarities and gauge whether or not your photo is of the same period.

This photograph is of a lady in the 1850s. Comparing your photograph with a similar one will give you clues as to whether to look before or after this period.

- ❧ Look at skirt, where is the waistline, is there a bustle.
- ❧ Are the sleeves long, straight or puffed?
- ❧ Is the neckline high or low?
- ❧ What kind of collar or fichu is worn?

FASHION RESOURCES FOR DATING PHOTOS

There are a number of websites that have detailed charts of fashion of from the early 19th Century through to the present.

When you are looking to identify a fashion era, only use the fashion charts of British and Australian fashions for Australian photographs as the fashions in the USA were quite different from ours. Our fashions, particularly female fashions, predominately followed British trends.

For example, the chart below shows fashions in Australia from 1860s - 2010s. By comparing your photo with these you can take a good guess at the time period of a photograph and research fashion in more detail.

Fashion History 1860 - 2020

Digital Art / Drawings & Paintings / Political©2013-2019 ArsalanKhanArtist

The following websites have useful charts and information for British clothing styles of various periods.

Victoria and Albert Museum - search for *textiles and fashion* on the search page https://collections.vam.ac.uk

My Modern Met - has a wonderful pictorial history of women's clothing.

https://mymodernmet.com/womens-fashion-history/

ADD YOUR OWN RESOURCES HERE

DATING NON-PORTRAIT PHOTOS

From 1888, when Kodak invented the first photographic film and paper, photography began to grow in popularity with ordinary people. With the release of the Kodak Box camera in 1900 it was possible to take and develop and print your own photos at home. Studio portraits began to make way for family photographs. It wasn't too long before colour photography came along. The formal setup of a photograph doesn't help with these. But clothing still can. (Women's hats are a great dating aid!)

In dating non-portrait photographs it becomes more important than ever to look closely at all of the photograph, not simply the subject.

Remember this fellow on the opposite page? He is my ancestor. When I first came across this photo my mother identified him as her grandfather, Grandpa Tom, and I thought,

' This is Great Grandpa John Thomas Dawson. He was an old man when this was taken and it was taken in his shed at the time of the coronation of Edward VII, about 1902.' I believed this for many years, until I examined the photo using the right dating techniques.

EXAMINE THE BACKGROUND;

- ℬ There's a workbench, and to the left is a string of some sort of mechanical parts.
- ℬ Above the bench a banner says 'God Save the Queen', not King. Queen Victoria must have been alive.
- ℬ Pinned to the banner are two photographs one of a man and the other a woman. This is a royal couple, and a Royal celebration, but could not be the coronation of 1902. I recognise the photos of the royal couple, they are the same photos as those on the family 1902 Guild souvenirs, celebrating the coronation of Edward VII and Queen Alexandra.
- ℬ In 1897 the Prince and Princess of Wales, Edward and Alexandra visited Preston in June to lead Queen Victoria's Diamond Jubilee celebrations. They were a tremendously popular couple.
- ℬ In the foreground, what I had thought were tables with cloths on them for a party are actually weaving frames, those found in a cotton mill. This is a jubilee celebration in a cotton mill. I can now date this photograph to approximately June, 1897.
- ℬ Put Great Grandpa back in the photo and look at him carefully.
- ℬ He is wearing oil stained trousers. In his hand is a large tool, similar to a screwdriver. This man, a grandparent of mine, is at work in a cotton mill in 1897.
- ℬ John Thomas Dawson was born in 1847. He would only have been 50 in 1897. This person appears much older than 50.
- ℬ This is not a photograph of Great Grandpa John Thomas Dawson. It could not be. The time period makes this person too old to be him.

This photograph is of my *Great Great* Grandpa, Thomas Blackledge, who was still working in the cotton mill as a machine mechanic at the age of 87, during the celebration of the Jubilee, and who died in November of that same year. This is the last known photo taken of him. Family legend called him Grandpa Tom. The photo when handed down was said to be a photo of Grandpa Tom. What my mother did not know was that it was her Great Grandfather on her Grandmother's side of the family - the Blackledges, also a family of Lancashire cotton weavers.

Photographs, when carefully examined, can yield a great deal of information.

MILITARY PHOTOGRAPHS

A clear photograph of a member of the armed forces can shorten the time and expense involved in searching military records. Badges on military uniforms change throughout military service, and can help identify and date portrait photographs.

BADGES

Metal or cloth badges are a key element of military uniforms. They are worn on a cap, collar, shoulder, arm, or cuff. They identify the rank of the person, their particular regiment or ship, qualification or specialist trade, and distinguish those with gallantry awards. They denote the Brigades, Divisions or Armies within which their unit is currently serving. Portrait photographs from World War I, such as the one opposite, were unofficial - the British Army did not photograph its First World War recruits. The images were typically taken while the soldier was on the first leave after being fitted with a uniform. They were given to loved ones or exchanged with friends.

It is a good idea to scan the photograph of the soldier at a very high resolution, 300dpi+, and then zoom in on those things that tell you where that person was, what armed force he/she belonged to, what unit and possibly what rank they held. The insignia on the service uniform are the indicators.

In this photograph of Joe Dawson, opposite, for example, zooming in on the insignia tells us quite a bit. When part of the photo is enlarged, we can see clearly that this person is sitting in front of a trench.

In the trenches of World War I, in the midst of battle, Joe would have been risking sure death. One of his mates is peering over the edge. He doesn't seem too worried about being shot either. They both look healthy and the uniform looks brand new. It's likely that this photo was taken in training camp, prior to embarkation. What is sure is that Joe was a World War I recruit.

The ammunition belt around his body tells us that he is a rifleman. His hat is on his knee and the hat badge is clearly in view.

Zooming in on the badge gives us an image we can research to find which unit of the armed forces he had enlisted in.

A Google search of 'British Army hat badges WWI' yields a bank of images to search through. Matching the Google image with the hat badge reveals Joe was in the Royal Artillery. It's now possible to go straight to the military records to search for details of Joe's WWI service.

These websites help with the identification of military insignia.

- ஐ https://www.iwm.org.uk/history/military-uniform-badges-and-portrait-photographs
- ஐ http://www.diggerhistory.info/pages-badges/corps.htm
- ஐ http://www.diggerhistory.info/pages-badges/navy_badges.htm
- ஐ http://www.diggerhistory.info/pages-badges/raaf2.htm

Make use of any photos you have of soldiers, airmen, sailors, nurses and other service men and women to give you a starting point in searching military records.

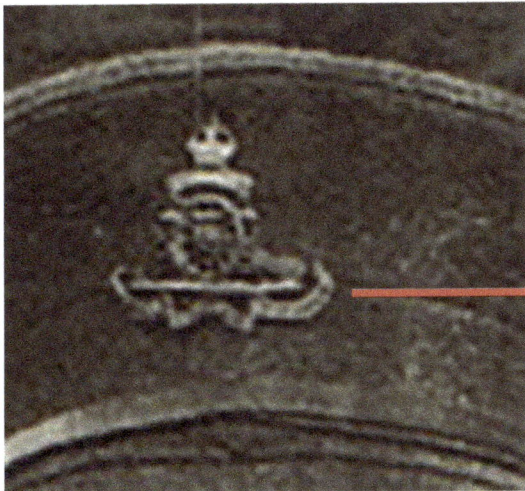

OUR PLACE

In this section you will learn;

- ∞ How to place your ancestors geographically and in time
- ∞ How to find them in census and other types of records
- ∞ How to expand the definition of place by connecting it with senses, memory and experience.
- ∞ How to use maps as a research tool.

WHAT DO WE MEAN BY PLACE?

Usually 'place' means a specific area or location. 'Place' can be as small as a spot on a shelf to as large as a region or country. Geographers, philosophers and artists challenge the usual meaning of place. Contrasting 'place' with 'space', they show us that 'place' is not only a designated area within the what we know as a space but that 'place' contains memories, experiences and associations that come with being *in place*. Humans are always in place. We come into the world and keep returning to it. Our understanding of place is impossible to separate from the sensations produced in that place - its sights, smells, textures, sounds and tastes. Some places also evoke an emotional response based on our experiences, memories and nostalgia.

Think about how our sense of place is built through stories and conversations:

- ∞ What stories about place are significant in your family?
- ∞ How can you capture the complexity of place through the multiple perspectives ad memories contained with your family?
- ∞ Think about how you can share memories about places of significance to you and your family?

Spending time in places, using our senses to explore and gain knowledge of them, allows us to come to know them intimately. Some families stay in their place forever, others move.

If they have moved, look for clues as to why. The reasons why people move can be strongly connected to place. Bad harvest and famines force some families to move, while new industries and opportunities such as gold rushes and land grants can draw people to new places.

Families may deliberately choose to move to places that remind them of the places they left behind; similarities in climate and/or natural and built environment. The move may be a radical shift in the experience of place - from crowded cities to isolated rural locations, from cold to hot, from spacious homes to small townhouses, terraces or apartments.

Moving and experiences of place are integral to family and community. They can be on a large scale, with whole villages moving together in voyages across the world or families seeking out groups from the same culture.

Finding out where family members lived, as well as when and where they moved, is a vital part of family history research. Putting people in place allows you to fill in the story of their lives, as well as providing leads to further resources and documentation.

Census records are created by governments to count the people living within a particular area. Censuses have also been taken by bodies such as churches and individuals.

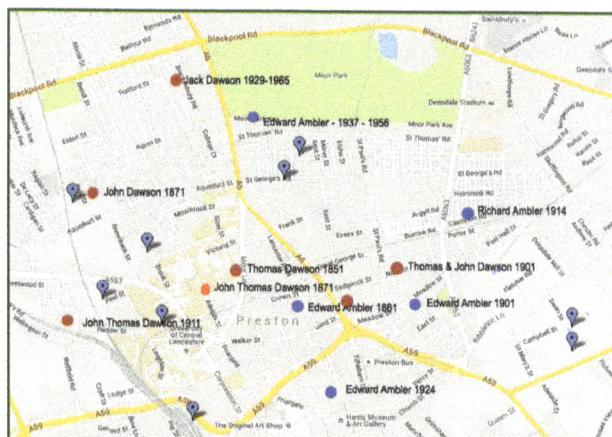

ENVIRONMENT

When building a picture of our ancestors' lives, it is impossible to understand why they made certain decisions, what their daily life would have been like or what opportunities they might have had for work or leisure without understanding the environment in which they lived, and how that might, or must, have interacted with it. This can include such influences as the politics and events of the time. Humans live in various environments;

    ⁖ Domestic spaces (houses and homes)

    ⁖ Community spaces (workplaces, marketplaces, pubic services, sites of community activity)

    ⁖ Cultivated spaces (agricultural land)

    ⁖ Wild or natural spaces

Documents, e.g. deeds, house plans, and photographs of built homes can be used to give an approximate date at which to start looking for an ancestor. In Australia, the characteristics are;

The late 19th and 20th centuries;

    ⁖ Terrace and inner-city housing

    ⁖ Workers living close to major centres of employment such as factories.

    ⁖ High density housing

    ⁖ Relatively little privacy within domestic spaces,

    ⁖ Limited amounts of green space within each property, and

    ⁖ The placement of services such as laundry and rubbish towards the rear of the house.

The rise of the ideal of the 'garden city' in the mid 20th Centuries ;

    ⁖ development of suburbia

    ⁖ more widely spaced housing

    ⁖ a healthier and more restful environment

    ⁖ the quarter-acre block

    ⁖ space for productive use and individual expression in the use of space

    ⁖ transportation networks and the increasing importance of private cars was mirrored in the design of suburban housing.

Developments in suburban living in the late 20th and 21st Century;

    ⁖ an increase in the size of the house footprint

    ⁖ greater expectations for privacy and personal domestic spaces and

    ⁖ a professionalisation of leisure and aspirational lifestyles framed by popular culture (such as renovation reality television).

LINKING FAMILY TO PLACE

The very earliest censuses happened in ancient times but for genealogical purposes an early census of interest is that of Iceland in 1703 which recorded the name, age, residence, and social standing of every inhabitant; an index of this census is available.

It is usual for censuses to be taken every 10 years, though some areas hold them on a 5 year cycle. Again, this frequency can change over time so do check your area of interest.

For family historians, they are very useful as they place your ancestors in a given location at a particular time. They usually show people in family groups. This may reveal relationships and previously unknown family members. They may include information on occupations, parental origin, year of migration, ability to read and write, religious affiliation and much more.

Census' are primarily created so that governments know how many people are living in the area of enumeration. This helps with issues of funding allocation and to assess the number of legislators required for an area.

Perhaps more interestingly, the characteristics of a population are also assessed, and this is where we get information such as whether a person could speak or write a particular language, the value of any life insurance held, whether a person was deaf and so on. All of this information gives the government a snapshot of its population and thus could help answer particular issues of concern.

Some countries do not keep (or have not kept for particular years) the individual/family details taken as part of census enumeration, thus all that is available to us are the statistical outcomes. These can be interesting as they give a flavour of the area in which your ancestors lived but no information on a particular person will be available.

It is important to find out who was supposed to be included in a household, as this varies

country to country and from time period to time period. In some places, only those staying in the residence on the census night were to be counted in that household and in others those who were 'normally resident' were to be counted. Knowing this may change your understanding of who you thought would be on the census at that address.

In Australia, the earliest systematic collection of data that linked people and place occurred in 1788. The Convict Musters were a count of everyone who had arrived in the colony aboard a convict transport, where they were living and to whom they had been assigned for work.

A Census conducted in New South Wales in 1828 became the first in a regular series in that colony and periodic censuses were taken in the other Australian colonies. The first simultaneous censuses of all the Australian colonies were taken in 1881 - this also formed part of the first simultaneous Census of the British Empire.

The first national Census for Australia was taken in 1911. This national Census was followed by others in 1921, 1933, 1947, 1954 and 1961. Since 1961 censuses have been conducted at five-yearly intervals.

However, in Australia, after the 1901 Census, census forms were destroyed once the statistical analysis was completed. No records for individuals survive. This was government policy up until 1996.

Note: No records of individuals exist for censuses after these dates:

- ఴ Victoria: 1853
- ఴ New South Wales: 1901
- ఴ Northern Territory: 1921
- ఴ Queensland: 1841
- ఴ South Australia: 1841
- ఴ Tasmania: 1857
- ఴ Western Australia: 1837

CONVICT MUSTER OF 1828

General Muster of Male & Female Convicts in the Colony of

Convicts Names		Name of the Ship in which they arrived	When	Where Tried
Corry Bartholomew	25	Lady McNaughton	1830	
Cassidy James	24	Roslyn Castle	"	
Clegg Joseph	35	Florentia	"	
Cavenor Thomas	29	Exmouth	1831	
Costello Michael	34	Sizemore	"	
Cussick John	42	Forth	1835	
Callaghan John	73	Britannia	1796	
Cass Edward	33	Hive	1833	
Collins John	23	Burrell	1831	
Crossley William	18	Lord Lyndock	1833	
Callegan Joseph	17	"	"	
Cutler Hugh	27	Hercules	1829	
Cousens Thomas	35	Countess Harcourt		
Coleham William	33	Granada	1819	
Calderwood John	39	Prince George	1824	
Collins James	37	Mangles	1833	
Chambers Joseph	26	Heighley	1834	
Cox William	45			
Cook John		Norfolk		
Colbeck George	21	Inverness	1833	
Chipps William	33	Roslyn Castle	1834	
Cavenagh L.	43	Cambury	1827	
Bruckbell John	57	Portland	1822	
Clark Thomas	16	Susan	1836	
Carroll Michael	24	Surry	"	
Connelly Owen	23		"	
Clark Charles	19	Reeves	"	
Cope William	20	Susan	"	
Collins Edward	19	Reeves	"	
Cotton Peter	40	Kennedy	1830	
Carney John	40	Forth	1829	
Cunningham David	30	Eliza	1830	

After statistical analysis was completed, typically census forms containing information about individuals were destroyed. For example, in 1892 all surviving Victorian household forms from earlier censuses were pulped. Earlier, in 1882, a fire destroyed the New South Wales census records for 1846, 1851, 1856, 1861, 1871 and 1881, including the household forms from 1861, 1871 and 1881.

A guide to Australian colonial census and muster records is available at the State Library of Victoria.

OTHER COUNTRIES

For those searching for their ancestors pre-transportation/emigration, the available UK and European Census records are a goldmine. Not only do they provide the name of the person you are researching, but every person who was in the dwelling with him/her on the day of the Census.

On the opposite page is an example of a 1911 UK Census Record.

You can access United Kingdom census records from 1841-1911 online.

UK Census Online is a free name and year search but requires a subscription to view the full details. British Census records are available for 1841, 1851, 1861, 1871, 1881, 1891, 1901, 1911.

Alternatively a search of all UK Census records can be made if you have a subscription to Ancestry.com.au or use the library edition of Ancestry.com at your local library.

New Zealand has no available Census Data on individuals. Convict musters can be found in the NSW State Records convict collection.

Searches of Census records are possible through Ancestry.com or Find My Past.

Both of these services require a subscription unless you are using the library edition of Ancestry through your local library.

Family Search has Census collections from a number of countries and is a free search for members.

For example;

1700s

Austria, Upper Austria, Wels, Census Records, 1613-1900

Central America, Colonial Records, 1607-1902

Finland, Church Census and Pre-Confirmation Books, 1657-1915

Germany, Bavaria, Middle Franconia, Brenner Collection of Genealogical Records, 1550-1900

Japan Census Records, 1661-1875

Netherlands Census and Population Registers, 1574-1940

Spain, Province of Gerona, Municipal Records, 1566-1956

1800 - 1849

Canada

Manitoba

Ontario

Caribbean and Central America

Continental Europe

South America

United States of America

1850 - 1899

Canada

Caribbean and Central America

Continental Europe

South America

United Kingdom and Ireland

United States of America

1900-1949

Caribbean and Central America

Continental Europe

Mexico

Pacific Islands

United States of America

CENSUS OF ENGLAND AND WALES, 1911.

Before writing on this Schedule please read the Examples and the Instructions given on the other side of the paper, as well as the headings of the Columns. The entries should be written in ink.

The contents of the Schedule will be treated as confidential. Strict care will be taken that no information is disclosed with regard to individual persons. The returns are not to be used for proof of age, as in connection with Old Age Pensions, or for any other purpose than the preparation of Statistical Tables.

Number of Schedule 103
(To be filled up by the Enumerator.)

NAME AND SURNAME	RELATIONSHIP to Head of Family.	AGE (last Birthday) and SEX		PARTICULARS as to MARRIAGE.						PROFESSION or OCCUPATION of Persons aged ten years and upwards.					BIRTHPLACE of every person.	NATIONALITY of every Person born in a Foreign Country.	INFIRMITY.
		Ages of Males	Ages of Females	State whether "Single," "Married," "Widower," or "Widow."	Completed years the present Marriage has lasted	Children born alive to present Marriage			Personal Occupation.	Industry or Service with which worker is connected.	Whether Employer, Worker, or Working on Own Account.	Whether Working at Home			
						Total Children Born Alive	Children still Living	Children who have Died								
Ambler Robert	Head	53		Married 23	23	4	3	1	Shopkeeper	Boots Manufy Worker				Preston Lancs Retford	do	
Ambler Mary A.	Wife		55	Married 23	23	4	3	1	Housekeeper					do do	do	
Ambler Robert	Son	20		Single					Shoemaker					Bur Ireland Ireland	do	
Ambler Grace	Daughter		19	do					Tailoress					Preston Lancs	do	
Ambler Edward	Son	17		do					Clerk Railway Rly					do	do	
Ambler Harold	Son	14		do					Apprentice Plumber					do	do	

	Total		
	Males	Females	Persons
(To be filled up by the Enumerator)	4	2	6

Initials of Enumerator M.M.S.

(To be filled up by, or on behalf of, the Head of Family or other person in occupation, or in charge, of this dwelling.)

Write below the Number of Rooms in this Dwelling (House, Tenement, or Apartment). Count the kitchen as a room but do not count scullery, landing, lobby, closet, bathroom; nor warehouse, office, shop.

Six

I declare that this Schedule is correctly filled up to the best of my knowledge and belief

Signature Robert Ambler

Postal Address 30 St Ignatius Square

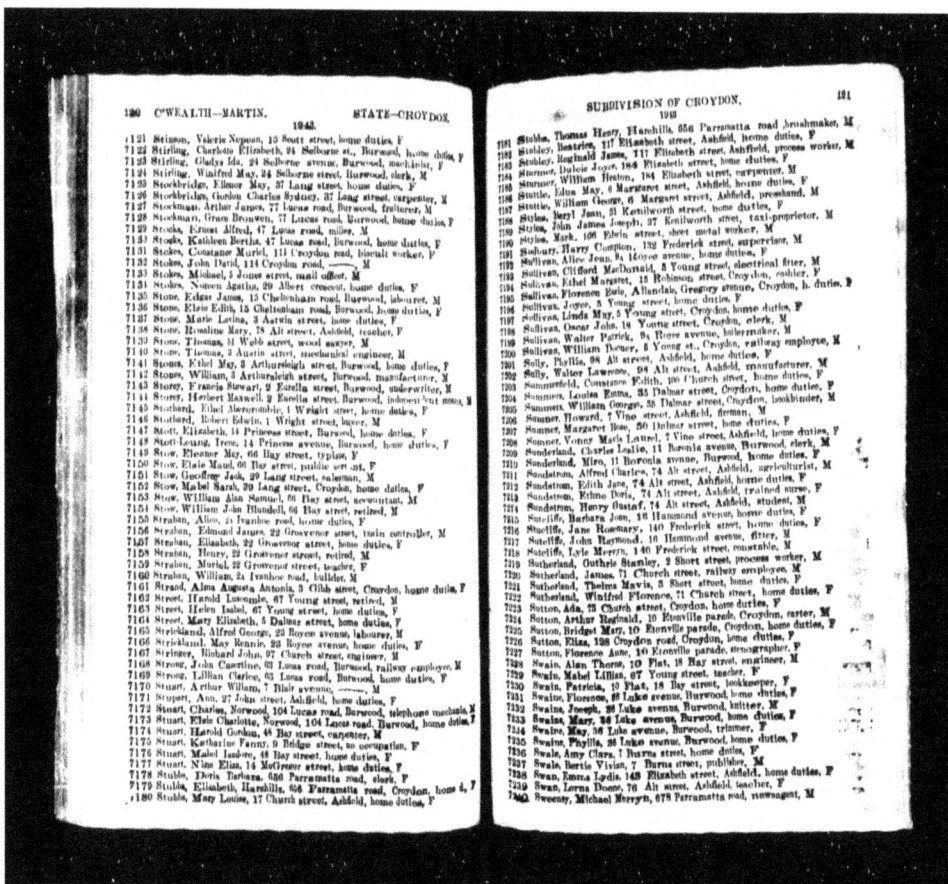

In the absence of census records, you can search alternative sources such as;

  ❧ electoral rolls,

  ❧ postal directories,

  ❧ phone and trade directories,

  ❧ council rate records,

  ❧ as well as documents such as birth, death and marriage records that include addresses.

The State Library of New South Wales has a guide to researching electoral rolls that includes a chronology of who had the vote.

Putting people in place enables us to think of them as members of a community. When we take part in community activities, both work and play, we leave an archival trail. Community groups that may be relevant to your search for your ancestors include:

  ❧ religious and church groups including charitable organisations and temperance societies

  ❧ ethnic groups

  ❧ service clubs such as Rotary, Lions, and city/suburb/town improvement associations

  ❧ trade and industry groups including unions

  ❧ special interest groups such as sports clubs, walking groups, and craft groups

  ❧ associations such as the Country Women's Association, Scouts and Guides, Rural Youth Clubs

  ❧ Masons and the Independent Order of Odd Fellows

  ❧ political groups

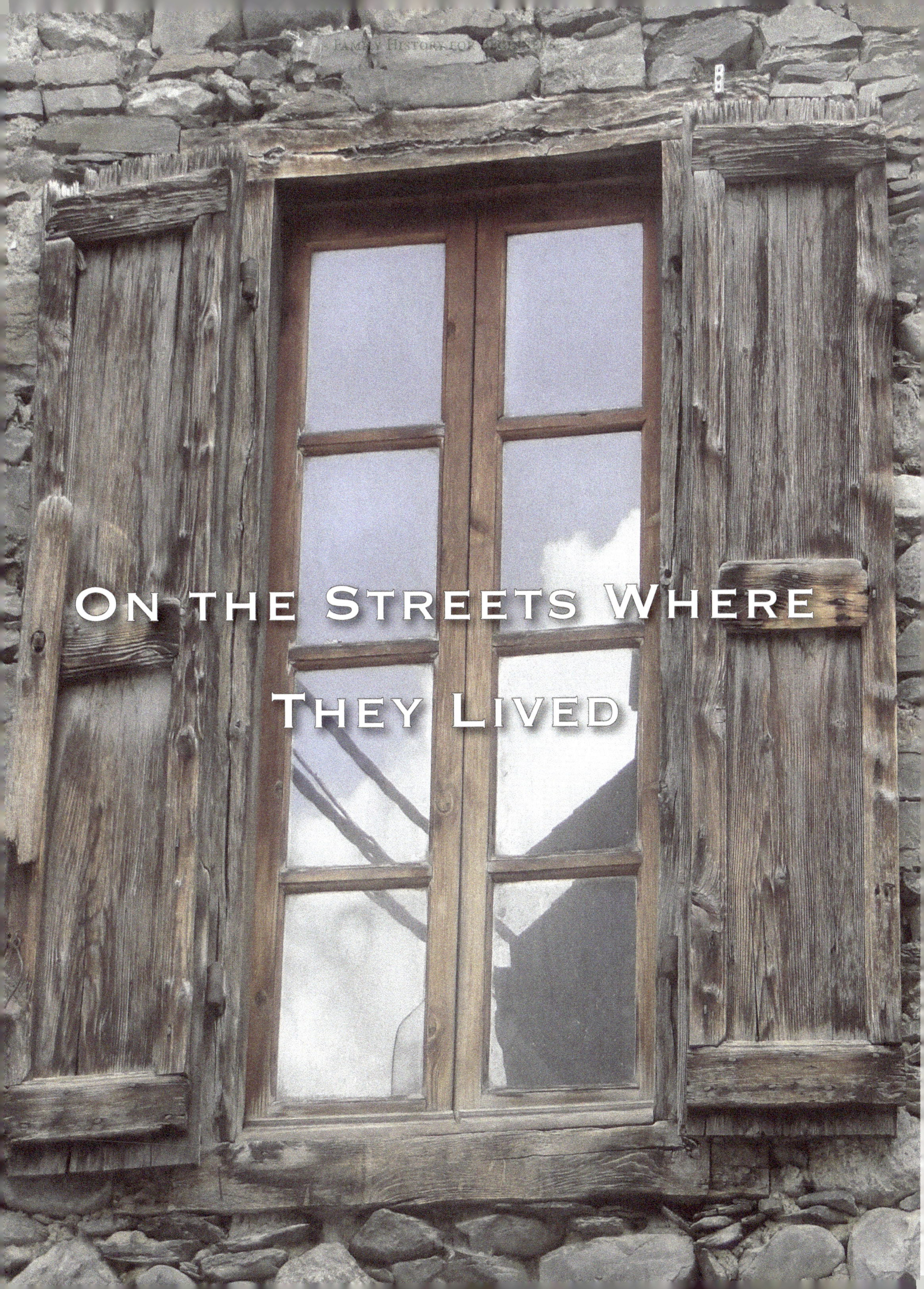

On the Streets Where They Lived

MAPS

Maps play an important role in both representing and moving around location. Maps encode knowledge of a location that can then be interpreted for use. There are six types of map.

- ℘ Political Maps: Political maps are the maps that you see most of the time. They focus on the boundaries, cities, states, and capitals. They show no topographical features.

- ℘ Physical Maps: Physical maps show the physical landscape of a place. They show things like mountains, rainforests rivers, and lakes. The elevation may be shown by a change in colour. Low elevations are shown in green and high elevations are shown in blue. They show very few cities.

- ℘ Topographical Maps: Two-dimensional representations of the earth's surface, such as vegetation, height or 'relief', water, and cultural features like roads and buildings. These maps are usually detailed and accurate in their use of scale.

- ℘ Climate Maps: Climate maps show information about the climate in specific area. They are usually differentiated by temperature or climate (like rainforest, desert, etc.) using different colours.

- ℘ Economic or Resource Maps: Economic or resource maps are used for tracking an economic activity or natural resource in an area though shapes, symbols, or colours.

- ℘ Road Maps: Road maps are used to show major and minor highways, roads, airports, city locations, and points of interest like parks.

- ℘ Informational Maps: Maps can also be snapshots of history.

Some maps are so much more than we understand a map to be: they show the course of discovery and place-naming. In some cases they're the first record of a land that's totally unknown to people from other places or they reveal specific aspects of an age of discovery.

Mapping can be a way of getting to know a place: surveying and map making using European tools and methods assisted in the colonisation of Australia. Maps from Australia's colonial history show land use, settlements and cultural groups that no longer exist.

In the early 20th Century, Daisy Bates drew 45 maps. They capture details of indigenous social groups, place names and land features such as waterholes, ranges and lakes.

Eddie Mabo's maps, created to support the formal recognition of native title, were hand-drawn on lined notepaper and shaded with coloured felt-tip pens. They show the traditional ownership boundaries of the Murray Islands in Torres Strait.

About 1910/12, a river pilot sketched a map of the Darling River Shoals on a piece of calico (opposite).

Using historic maps can give us an insight into a place at different stages of its development. Historic maps also enable us to locate addresses and locations relevant to family history research and put them into a wider context of place.

However, streets can vanish over time, renamed, or subsumed into housing or industrial developments. The Scottish National Archives has a facility whereby you can find the address of your ancestors on an old map and overlay on a modern map, thus being able to identify its current geographical location. You can find this on old Maps Online or through the Archives.

Old Maps Online is a website that draws together old maps from a range of libraries, museums, universities and other institutions. It brings together maps from different periods, so you can find the map with the date range most relevant to your family history.

One of Eddie Mabo's hand drawn maps. Edward Koiki Mabo   nla.gov.au/nla.cat-vn878792

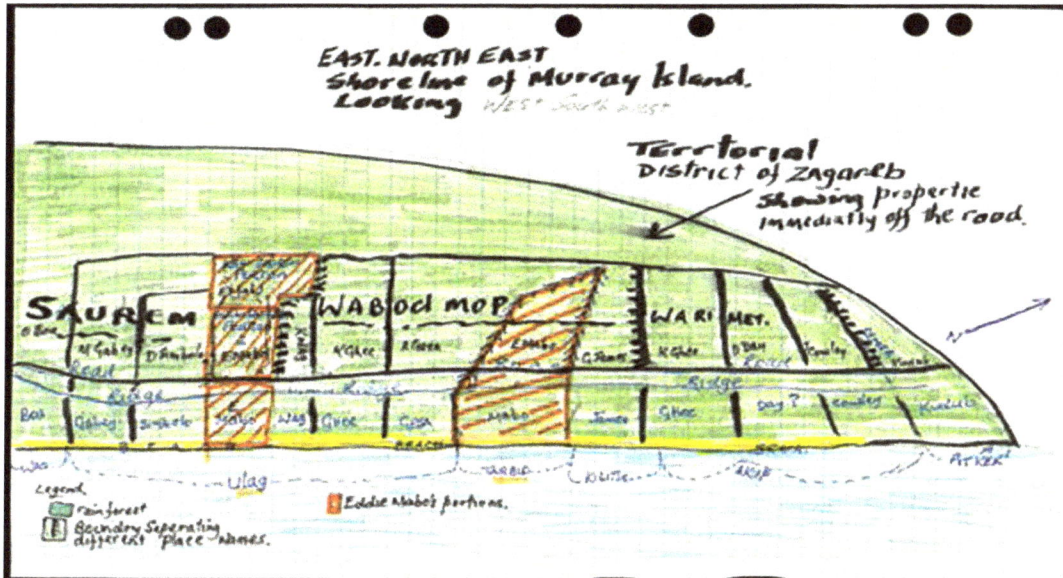

Darling River pilot chart, circa 1912-17.

This calico drawing shows the shoals upstream of Wentworth, NSW. (NLA)

Sydney City Rail System map pre-Airport Line.

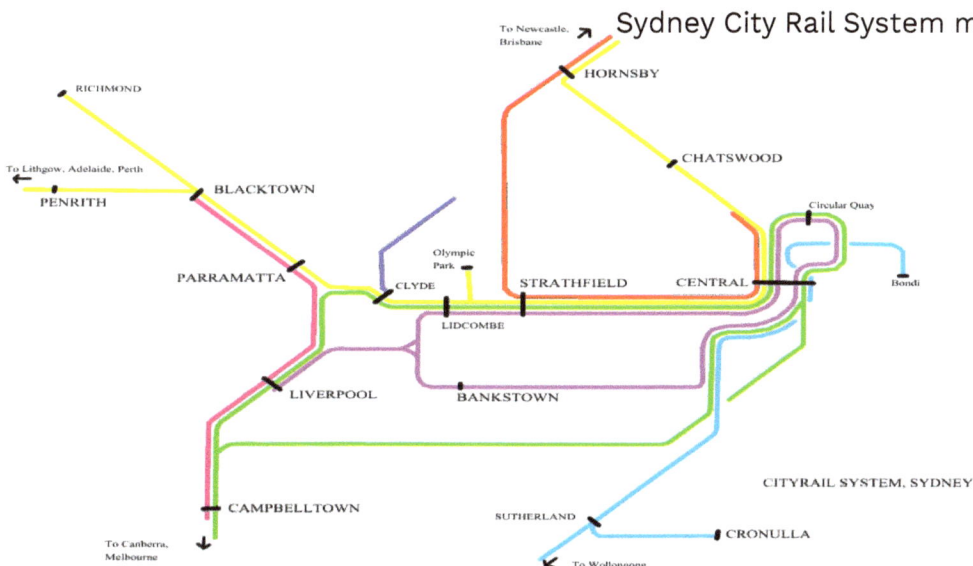

THEIR PLACE IN TIME

Maps created of the same place at different times in its history can tell stories of a family's history over time. For example, in trying to understand the movements of the Dawson family, weavers of Preston in the north of England, I used maps to trace the family as it moved from street to street through the town.

Maps were an integral part of getting to know my ancestor from a different viewpoint.

However, maps were not the only resource needed to come to this understanding. I also needed to investigate the times through which each generation lived and worked to see the influences that environment had upon them.

TIME

Finding out where family members lived at a particular time is a crucial part of family history research. Identifying if and when they moved and why, or what they were doing at a specific time, adds depth to their story, and often raises more questions.

Understanding the time in which an ancestor lived and how this might have influenced their way of life, where they lived and what they did to survive - their work or actions - requires a broader historical research.

The sources that can be used are;

NEWSPAPERS OF THE TIME.

Letters to the editor are invaluable and the shipping news can tell stories of migration and trade.

HISTORY BOOKS

Remembering always that history is written and/or interpreted from a biased perspective. Make sure you check the credentials of the authors and publishers.

LITERATURE

Books written at the time or by people who are the trusted storytellers of a region.

Preston in the 1840s and 50s was the "Coketown" of Charles Dicken's novel "Hard Times" and gives a very good picture of the environment of the cotton town and its 'dark satanic mills'.

There is a book, "Tales From Barra Told by the Coddie", published in 1992, that gave me the history, mythology, culture and folklore of my Barra & McNeil ancestors that I have been unable to find anywhere else.

DOCUMENTARIES

Videos and films, particularly early documentary movies can be a valuable source of information about how people lived in the early years of the 20th century.

For example, there is a series of movies made in the 1920s in the Outer Hebrides that shows a women's way of life that no longer exists in the remote islands of Scotland. It gave me an understanding of my 3x Gr Grandmother's way of life; her daily work, her songs, her language, that I could not have found any other way.

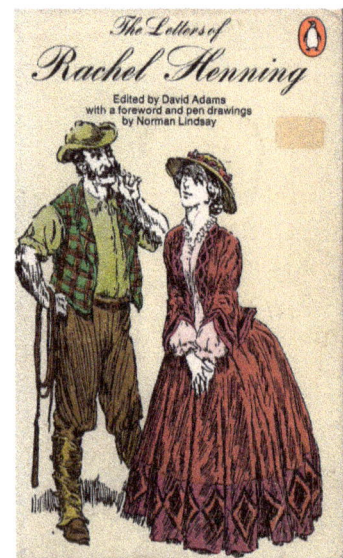

The Letters of
Rachel Henning
Edited by David Adams
with a foreword and pen drawings
by Norman Lindsay

USING NEWSPAPERS AND JOURNALS

There is no better place to look for a clear picture of life and times than in the newspapers of the day. Newspapers have sections that yield informations about all manner of facets of life, for example;

- 📖 Newspaper reports of important events
- 📖 Letters to the editor reveal local conflict as well as attitudes and values and politics of the time
- 📖 Classified advertisements can reveal a trade or business or give you an indication of the cost of living
- 📖 Newspaper photos show you the environment
- 📖 Court reports can lead to tracking down convict ancestors
- 📖 Shipping movements tell you of trade in and out of local ports and often of shipwrecks and passenger details.
- 📖 Family notices can reveal information about family members and in-law relationships through birth, marriage, death and engagement notices.

Access is available;

- 📖 to Australian papers through Trove and is a free online service https://trove.nla.gov.au
- 📖 to the UK papers through https://www.britishnewspaperarchive.co.uk
- 📖 through Ancestry.com

Newspapers are invaluable in understanding a family's place in time.

These newspaper accounts are from the "Lancashire Evening Post" between 1890 and 1910.

The first reveals that my 2x Great Grandfather, Edward Ambler, served on the Grand Jury at the Quarter Sessions, of which I was unaware.

PRESTON EPIPHANY QUARTER SESSIONS.

These sessions were opened on Wednesday last, at the Court House, House of Correction, before Mr. T. B. Addison, chairman, and several other magistrates.

The calendar contained the names of fifty-four prisoners for trial—forty-four of whom were charged with felony, and ten with misdemeanour. The educational analysis showed that twelve could neither read nor write, twenty-eight could read and write imperfectly, three could read and write well, ten could read only, and the educational status of one was undescribed.

THE BAR.—The following gentlemen of the bar were in attendance:—Messrs. Knowles, Catterall, Kay, Dawson, Gardner, Dwyer, Sidgreaves, Pope, Rostron, Watson, Addison, James, Eccles, Segar, Gorst, and Makinson.

GRAND JURY.—The following gentlemen composed the grand jury:—Mr. Thomas Threlfall, Preston, foreman; Messrs. E. Ambler, W. Catterall, T. Atkinson, H. Charnley, G. Wilding, and W. Poole, Preston; Messrs. Jonas Bradley, James Spencer Briggs, and Edward Cottam, Blackburn; Messrs. John Hargreaves, Robert Hornby, Richard Smith, William Townley, and Richard Varley, Clitheroe; Messrs. Thomas Smire, Lawrence Whittaker, junr., James Edward Worsley, and William Whittaker, Haslingden; Messrs. Wm. Grimshaw and Thos. Topper, Higham-with-West-Close-Booth; and Mr. William Hudson, Woodplumpton.

The second tells a story of the health risks for small children at that time.

The Registrar General reports that during the three months ending 30th September last, there were 1,110 births and 858 deaths registered in the district or union of Preston, and he adds that the latter total occurs against an average of 832, taken from the three previous corresponding periods. The deaths include 319 below 1, and 1,461 that occurred at 60 and upwards. There were 56 deaths registered in public institutions, 21 were enquired into by the coroner, and 19 were due to violence. With respect to the causes of death there is record made of 10 fatal cases of measles, 8 of scarlet fever, 12 of diphtheria, 13 of whooping cough, 19 of fever, 190 of diarrhœa, and 2 of simple cholera. Diarrhœa seems to have been unusually prevalent and fatal, even for the season, but the other items in this account denote a very good state, on the whole, of the public health in the district, scarlet fever has declined from 25 and 16 to 8, but other fevers have merely changed in the three quarters from 20 and 15 to 19. An examination of the local returns shows that 31 deaths were registered in Longton sub-district, 2 less than the average. Here scarlet fever caused 3 deaths and other fevers 2. In Preston sub-district the births were 853 and the deaths 650, the latter being 6 below the average. Here scarlet fever caused 5 and other fevers 13. In Walton-le-Dale sub-district the deaths were 51, 11 more than the estimate. One was referred to fever. In Alston sub-district the deaths were 37, 7 more than the average. One of these also resulted from fever. In Broughton sub-district the deaths were 89, 16 more than the average. Two of these were referred to fever. The various local

CASE STUDY - TIME AND PLACE WORKING TOGETHER.

Placing people in both time and place allows you to fill in the story of your ancestors' lives, as well as giving you leads for accessing further resources and documentation. The further back in time you have to look, the harder it becomes to find records of your ancestor. Prior to about 1750, records were only kept of prominent people. There are references to those who were tenants on large estates or who held responsible positions in stately residences, but they are rare. However, if you can find your ancestor in time and place, research into the life and times of the populace in that period will give you some 'best guess' understanding of what their lives may have been like and why they made the choices that puzzle you. However, when you put maps, census records and the history of a town together it is possible to reveal the movements of a family over time, the reasons for their movements and the changes in their lifestyle brought about by political and social upheavals and a changing environment.

For example, my maternal ancestors were weavers, right back to the 18th century. They lived around the outskirts of Preston in the UK, employed in the weaving cottage industry. My paternal ancestors on the other hand were merchants. They had businesses as corn merchants, printers and administrators. The census showed me where they lived in the early 1800s and Google shows me where they live now. There would only be a matter of 2 miles (around a kilometre) difference, with the exception of my parents, my brother and me. We moved 12000 miles away, to Australia.

There are old maps available of a particular area in which my family lived in the late 1700s and still live today. Below is the Ordinance Map of Moor Park, Preston Circa 1829. There are no cotton mills adjacent to the park. Moor Park is open moorland where anyone may graze their animals and allotments are close by for people to grow vegetables. The cattle market is to the west and most dwellings to the east and south. There is minimal landscaping,

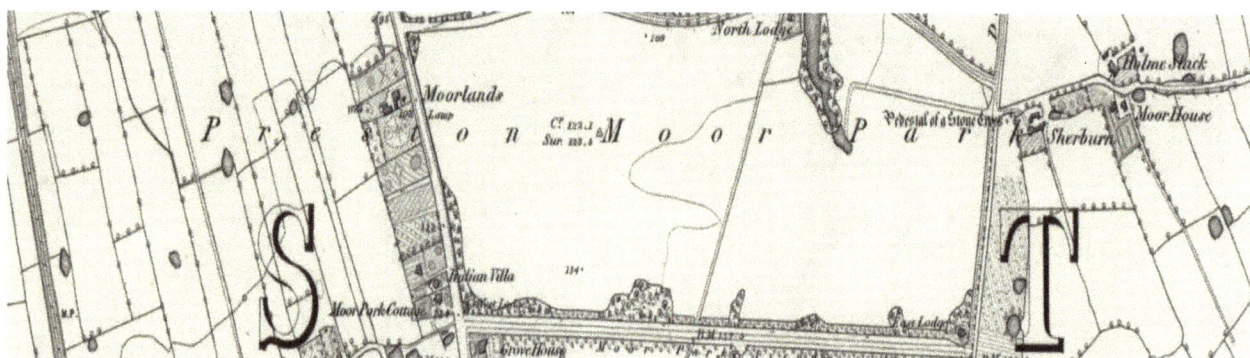

In another map of the 1850s, the environment has changed. Why? Cotton mills and workers cottages were starting to be built. The only open land was the moorland where anyone could graze their stock without fee. By the 1860s, the intensive housing required for workers who now worked in 50+ cotton mills that had opened in Preston had taken over all of available land in that area. Cottage industry was gone, the cotton industry had boomed.

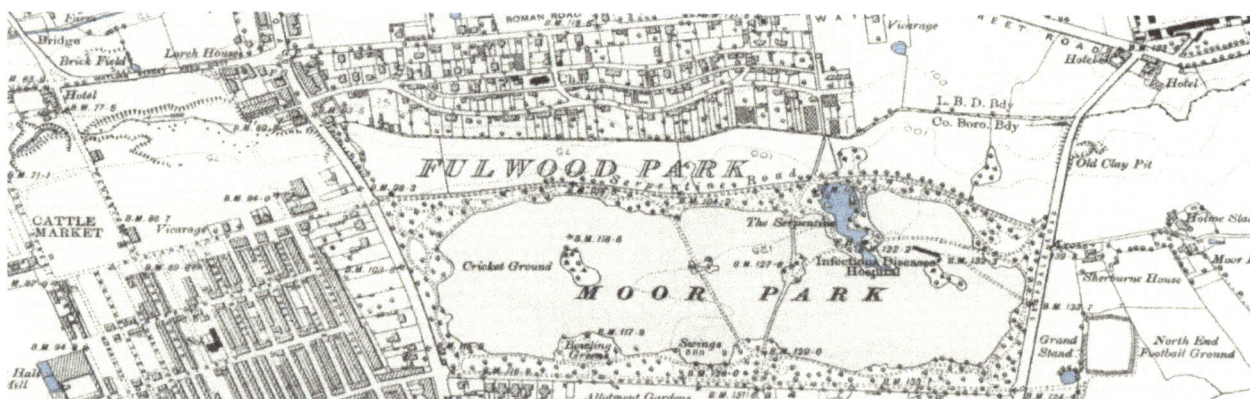

Over a period of 100 years this small area in which both the Amblers and the Dawsons lived changed from a semi-rural environment to an extension of the industrial cotton town. The weavers' terraces that sprang up in the 1850s were dark, with a "lobby" in between the homes and only a small back yard with an outside toilet serviced by the night-cart. The roads were cobblestoned and narrow and the drains ran with effluent. What had been open land, freely used by all for walking, grazing their stock and growing their food, gradually became an enclosed recreation area. Those who could afford it played tennis and bowls, strolled the landscaped walks and the more affluent lived in grand Victorian semi-detached homes built along the pleasant and well groomed Moor Park Avenue.

By 1929 Moor Park has become a recreation area with sports facilities and pleasant walks, landscaping and a leafy avenue leading from the east to the west and the southern end. The Park School is on the avenue and there is an open air school in the north east corner of the park. Mills have been built to the west, along with row upon row of 'two-up and two-down' terraces to provide cheap housing close to the mill for weavers.

Gradually towards the end of the 1890s the maps show that the moor became parkland, around which the wealthy built large Victorian homes. Garstang Road ran between the parklands and the workers terraces. By 1950 Garstang Road was a dividing line between the classes. Middle class on the Moor Park side and working class on the other.

I can trace the movements of my mother's Dawson ancestors to the working area close to Moor Hall Mill. They move from mill to mill, as a larger one opened up they moved closer. In 1950, when the cotton mills began to close down, they were living in the workers terraces on Brackenbury Street, parallel with Garstang Rd. In the 1960s, as British immigration from the West Indies and the Indian Subcontinent commenced, they moved away from there and into modern semi-detached housing further away from the now defunct mills.

The Amblers, my father's family, in the 1800 were printers and business owners. Over time they moved from flats over their business premises to rented and owned homes in more affluent areas of Preston. Some lived close to the sea in Lytham and others in the 'posh' areas of Penwortham, across the river. By 1950 my Ambler grandparents were living on Moor Park Avenue.

Set against the history of the industrial revolution and the gradual demise of the cotton industry, Moor Park is a focus point for setting my ancestors in time and place through maps, photographs and newspaper accounts. They helped to explain their differing lifestyles and the cultural and social divisions between them.

Tracing the movements of these two families across the old maps, reading the newspapers of the time, finding old photographs of the homes and buildings and plotting on old maps the changes over time in the built and natural environment gives me a greater understanding of why my two sets of grandparents rarely came together, and why my parents decided that emigration to Australia offered them a better future.

TIME AND PLACE REFERENCES

1. The Photograph and Australia: Timeline https://www.artgallery.nsw.gov.au/artsets/51b88k accessed Nov. 2018

2. Alexander, Alison Photography in Companion to Tasmanian History University of Tasmania, Hobart, Tasmania http://www.utas.edu.au/library/companion_to_tasmanian_history/P/Photography.htm

3. British Library Timelines; Invention of photography http://www.bl.uk/learning/timeline/item106980.html

4. Photographers of Great Britain and Ireland 1840 - 1940 http://www.cartedevisite.co.uk

5. Cyndi's List Photography https://www.cyndislist.com/photos/dating/

6. Parish and Historical maps of NSW - NSW Land Registry Services website https://www.nswlrs.com.au/Parish-and-Historical-Maps

7. Parish and County maps of Qld - https://www.qld.gov.au/recreation/arts/heritage/museum-of-lands/maps-plans/parish-country

8. Historical qld Maps https://www.qld.gov.au/recreation/arts/heritage/museum-of-lands/maps-plans

9. Qld Parish maps - https://publications.qld.gov.au/dataset/historical-parish-directoryqueensland

10. Qld Museum of Lands, Mapping and Surveying https://www.qld.gov.au/recreation/arts/heritage/museum-of-lands

11. Old Maps Online - Index of collections of historical maps from around the world. https://www.oldmapsonline.org

12. The Bureau of Meteorology Climate Data Online allows you to search for historic weather data, such as temperatures and rainfall, back to mid-1800s in some sites. http://www.bom.gov.au/climate/cdo/about/cdo-selecting-data.shtml

13. An easy-to-use facility for finding modern localities in Australia is the Geoscience Australia site here: http://www.ga.gov.au/map/names/.

14. Tourist maps. http://www.wilmap.com.au

15. The National Library of Australia have digitised a great many maps and plans able to be zoomed and panned. Use the search facility here: http://www.nla.gov.au/digicoll/maps.html. Includes maps and plans of real estate developments in NSW and Queensland.

16. National Library of Scotland: Map Images. https://maps.nls.uk

17. The National Library of Scotland's Map Library's website makes high resolution, zoomable maps of England, Scotland, Wales and beyond freely available. There are over 130,000 maps available from Ordnance Survey maps to Admiralty charts. A truly invaluable resource with an easy to use interface.

18. David Rumsey Map Collection. This privately owned historical map collection has over 65,000 maps and images freely availablehttps://www.davidrumsey.com/help/references

19. 1911 England Census Census Returns of England and Wales, 1911. Kew, Surrey, England: The National Archives of the UK (TNA), 1911. Data imaged from the National Archives, London, England.

ADD YOUR OWN REFERENCES HERE.

FREE BRITISH RESOURCES

1. *FamilySearch   www.familysearch.or*   Access the International Genealogical Index and thousands of parish registers, plus indexes to workhouse records, land tax assessments, school registers, court books, manorial documents and international records.

2. *Access to Archives   www.nationalarchives.gov.uk/a2a*   This catalogue describing archives held in hundreds of records offices is great for discovering names attached to deeds, insurance records, bastardy orders and more.

3. *The National Archives   www.nationalarchives.gov.uk/records/digital-microfilm.htm*   Download a selection of TNA's online records for free, including Women's Royal Naval Service officers' WW1 appointment registers, Coastguard records and Ministry of Health files about workhouse inmates and staff in series MH 12.

4. *National Library of Wales   www.llgc.org.uk*   Search 7.6 million articles from newspapers printed in English and Welsh between 1804 and 1919, find pre-1858 wills, gaol files for the Court of Great Sessions and applications for marriage licenses.

5. *National Library of Scotland   http://digital.nls.uk*   Browse British military lists and old maps, search Scottish Post Office directories by name and access genealogies of ancient Scottish families from the NLS Digital Gallery.

6. *National Archives of Ireland*   www.genealogy.nationalarchives.ie   Find surviving Irish censuses, probate calendars up to 1922, First World War soldiers' wills and the Tithe allotment books of 1823–1837.

7. *Public Record Office of Northern Ireland*   www.proni.gov.uk   Search Northern Irish Will Calendars, Valuation Revision Books, street directories, freeholders' records, war memorials, names on the Ulster Covenant and photographs.

8. *CWGC www.cwgc.org* The Commonwealth War Graves Commission database locates graves and memorials dedicated to service personnel and civilians who died in both world wars.

9. *The Gazette   www.thegazette.co.uk*   The official journal of records has been scanned from 1665 to the present day, containing published lists of bankrupts, military personnel mentioned in despatches and probate notices.

10. *Connected Histories   www.connectedhistories.org*   Hunt for ancestors who were clergymen, Londoners, transported convicts, witnesses at the Old Bailey and learn more about where they lived with the Victoria County History, Survey of London and Charles Booth Archive.

Dealing with the Family Treasures

THE FAMILY "STUFF"

People have complex relationships with 'things'. There are some that we consider dispensable and others that we treasure, keep and pass on to the next generation. If we have a strong sense of family, we may become 'hoarders', unwilling to part with anything that has family stories or memories attached to it. We hang onto Great Grandma's favourite books, Grandpa's false teeth, Uncle Albert's glass eye, and expect that the rest of the extended family will love them as much as we do.

Think about your own family collection:

- ଧ What is the scope of your family collection?
- ଧ What sorts of objects do you hold?
- ଧ Are they scarce or plentiful?
- ଧ Are there areas where you feel your family history is well represented?
- ଧ Are there gaps?
- ଧ How has your family collection developed?
- ଧ Have objects been passed down to you? If so, why and how?
- ଧ If you have had few or no objects passed down to you, how have you chosen to gather material relating to your family history?
- ଧ What is the relationship between the collection you hold and other collections within the family?
- ଧ Are objects distributed across a number of family members, or concentrated in a limited grouping of collections?
- ଧ Are objects relating to your family history held in by museums or other institutional collections? What level of access of you have to objects held outside your collection?
- ଧ How do you share your collection? What is your purpose in choosing to keep objects associated with your family history? What objects have you passed on or let go, and why?

Most family historians, besides being the keepers of the records, are also keepers of the 'stuff'; the photographs, heirlooms, bits and pieces handed down from generation to generation.

Why do we do this? Why do we hang onto all the old possessions of a bygone era and hand it on down the line?

Much of this can be explained as 'Collective memory'.

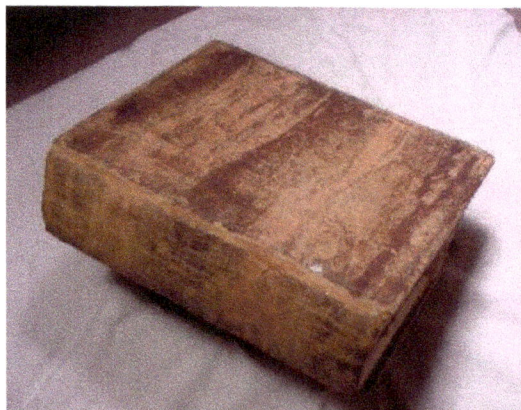

COLLECTIVE MEMORY

From artists to scientists, the process of making and recalling memories has been explored and studied. Although individual memories are based on unique individual experience, memories are strengthened, shaped and coloured through stories. As we retell our memories, these memories form a piece in the larger story of who we are.

Similarly, the retelling of past events as collective memories can shaped shared identities. Collective memories are the product of an evolving consensus among a group about its past. They alter over time. Families have their own collective memories: the stories that are passed down and retold. Sometimes these stories are serious, recollecting traumatic and difficult histories, but they can also be humorous and frivolous. Artefacts and images play a role in holding collective memory: they not only feature in these memories or document the events but also provide reminders and triggers for the retelling of these memories. The other reason we are so concerned about the family treasures is our nostalgia, which is quite different to memory.

NOSTALGIA

The term 'nostalgia' was originally coined to describe homesickness: a desire for a place left behind that was so strong it could appear as an illness. Over time, the meaning of nostalgia has slipped from being about a *place* left behind to a *time* left behind and childhood is a prime candidate for nostalgic longing.

The combination of memory and nostalgia causes us to be concerned about;

- ✺ Who will I hand this down to?
- ✺ Who will want it when I am gone?

All too often the answer is 'no-one'.

The sad fact is that the following generation have no interest in what they see as 'clutter' and 'old tatt'. It has no value to them unless the collective memory and nostalgia has been passed down to them before we are gone.

To value their heirlooms, they need to know the stories, know what it is, who had it and how, when, where and why it was in their possession. Too often the task of selecting what should be kept and what should be let go seems insurmountable. In approaching this, it is vital to have at the top of your mind the real significance of objects and images to the story in your family's history.

Ask yourself,

- ✺ Is it part of the proof of ancestry?
- ✺ Is it part of the evidence of when, how, why, what and where we came from?

Veronica Bullock says:

"We cannot keep everything forever. Therefore significance assessment is vital to make the best use of our scarce resources for collecting, conserving, documenting and digitising our collection materials.

Significance is not an absolute state - rather, it is relative, contingent and dynamic. Views on significance depend on perspective and can change over time."

There are three ways of looking at objects that will enrich our family history;

- ✺ Looking at our ancestors through their objects
- ✺ Looking at the history of our objects and
- ✺ Looking at our ancestors with their/our objects.

In telling the history of things, we take objects as the subject of historical enquiry. We look at specific objects or categories of objects. The object itself is important. It can also lead us to explore changes in technology and industry and the effect that these have had on our family's way of life and movements.

Objects can give us insights into both the personal and cultural histories of our forebears. For this reason, we need to understand how and why an object has been produced.

We need to think about the 'biography' of an object - what has happened to it through its use, how it has been kept and passed on, why it may have been discarded or re-purposed.

History from things uses objects to gain information about the past. This is obviously most useful where no written records survive.

Where there are archival documents, history from things can fill gaps in the written record. This may relate to people whose stories were not recorded, or recorded primarily for official purposes – e.g. convict records and migration documents.

It may also give insight into activities that are recorded; parts of everyday life, or where there is an unwritten ban on recording these activities.

Researching history and things at the same time places history and things side by side, emphasising that our possessions, our 'stuff' offer an understanding of the past as a material world. Interactions between people and things impact on both; we make them, they shape us.

The photograph below, together with the shuttle from one of machines, gives me a better understanding of my Great Grandmother's working life in the cotton mills of the late 1800s and early 1900s.

CONTEXTUAL ANALYSIS

Contextual analysis requires us to place an image or artefact in a particular cultural and historical context. Within that context, we may look to the social, economic, political, spiritual and institutional systems that play a role in how an image or object was made and understood.

It's important that we see images and objects not as a result of their context, but as taking an active role in influencing ideas, feelings and behaviours.

Contexts shift, as images and objects move through time and space.

You can see this in relation to your own family treasures: their significance and function change as they are passed across generations.

Some questions you might ask in a contextual analysis are:

- What motivated the production of the image?
- Was this a primarily individual act, or was there a patron, work or institutional environment that required it to be made?
- Is there any documentation that gives insight into these motivations? (This could range from a diary entry by an artist or photographer to an invoice or order.)
- Who was able to see this image or object? Under what circumstances?
- Is there any record of viewer reactions when it was shown?
- Does the choice of materials have meaning beyond their functional nature? Are they rare and costly, or common?
- Are the materials new and innovative? Do the materials have a symbolic value?
- What is the subject? Why would makers or viewers be interested in this subject?
- Is it conveying political, social or personal messages?

To find answers, you will need to look for evidence beyond the object itself. In many cases, the evidence will be incomplete or inconclusive there will be an element of interpretation and speculation.

Look at this photograph of the children of St Francis Catholic School in the UK (Circa 1954.
Ask some of the above questions about it. What would you need to know before you could answer them?

Researching and Recording

In Family History, as in all research, we move from the known to the unknown. Known really does mean KNOWN. In the case of objects, knowing them means knowing;

- What they are.
- How they were made and
- How they were used by anyone at all that owned them.

If we take a simple cup and saucer, as an example, knowing what it is made of, where it was made and its maker will lead to being able to date it and, if its origin in the family is unknown, give you at least a best guess as to who was its first family owner. This approach of moving from the unknown to the known is different to that used in document based research. Here is a guide to the process, a three-step process that you can use in analysing objects:

1. Write a description of the object, focusing on its physical attributes. The description might include size, weight, shape, decoration, and materials. If possible, note any visible information that tell you about how it was made. See if this initial investigation can give you a possible date for the object (or you may know this already).

2. Place the object in a historical context by bringing in other evidence. Questions to drive this stage of the investigation are;
   - Who owned this object (or similar objects)?
   - What was object used for?
   - How much would it cost for contemporaries and/or how much labour was involved in the processes of making the object?
   - What is the historical setting for this object?

3. Finally, we place the object in a socio-cultural context by thinking about the meanings, implications and values associated with the object. The sources you may need here can include images and 'imaginative' sources such as fiction writing, popular culture, and film and audio sources.

Applying Object Analysis

Let's see how this process of analysis has been applied to the example on the next page, a pair of cups and saucers that has been passed down through the Dawson family, my maternal ancestors.

I started my Object record with photos and a simple physical description of what you can see and tell by looking at it. A more detailed description of each cup and saucer set follows. The next step was to research how an image could be made to appear in the clay of the object. This meant searching the Internet and museum collections etc to find a similar object using the same process. The manufacturing process for these objects was identified as lithophane porcelain. The history of the object also includes a statement of the historical significance of the object and the events that brought about its creation.

Next, I related how these objects came into the Dawson family. This can only be a 'best guess' if there is not a record of its purchase or acquisition. The only source of information for these items was family oral history. Footnotes indicate the source of the information.

The final step in describing objects is a statement of significance, which is a thoughtful summary of the values, meaning and importance of an item in your collection. Writing a statement of significance draws on the research and evaluation of the item or collection that you have already carried out, and makes an argument for its significance to your family.

'GUILD AND CORONATION COMMEMORATIVE CUPS'

DAWSON FAMILY

A commemorative pair of cups and saucers of original antique Lithophane porcelain, created for the Preston Guild of 1902 and coronation of King Edward VII. Both are in excellent condition, with no chips or cracks but some wearing of the gilt due to age, washing and use.'

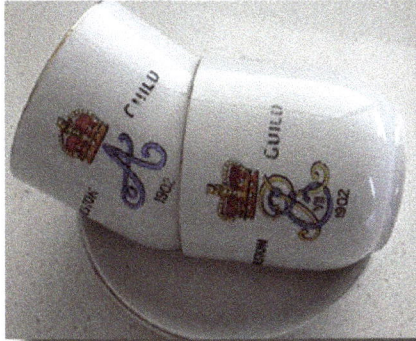

Set 1: The saucer is made of white porcelain, round in shape, with ring base, gilded at the rim and the edge of the ring. The cup is also of porcelain, round, 7cm tall and 5.7 cm diameter with an ear shaped loop handle. The obverse is decorated with the royal cypher, with stylised interlaced letters 'ERV II', surmounted by text 'Preston Guild 1902' and a gold and red crown. The rim is edged in gilt and the handle is gilded. When the cup is held to the light, it shows a hidden image of King Edward VII in the base.

Set 2. The saucer is made of white porcelain, round in shape, with ring base, gilded at the rim and the edge of the ring. The cup is also of porcelain, round, 7cm tall and 5.7 cm diameter with an ear shaped loop handle. The obverse is decorated with a stylised interlaced letter 'A', surmounted by text 'Preston Guild 1902' and a gold and red crown. The rim is edged in gilt and the handle is gilded. When the cup is held to the light, it shows a hidden image of Queen Alexandra in the base.

The images have been created using a lithophane process. Lithophane is a term derived from the Greek litho meaning stone and phainen meaning to cause to appear. They were first created in Europe in the 1820s. A lithophane is created through a process of etching or moulding artwork in very thin translucent porcelain that can only be seen clearly when back lit with a light source.

They began as an image carved in warm wax on a glass plate. This was then backlit. A modeller would duplicate the image on a flat wax plate carving relief and intaglio. Where the wax was carved thinnest, more light would shine through and where it was thickest less light shone through.

A plaster gypsum mould was then cast from the wax. The casts would include around 66% kaolin, 30% feldspar and 4% soapstone. The casts were removed from the moulds and then fired to about 2300 degrees Fahrenheit. Today lithophanes are made using CNC and CAD processes, greatly reducing the cost.

This object came into the possession of the Dawson family when it was acquired by Annie Noble, wife of John Noble during the Preston Guild of 1902. It has been handed down from mother to daughter since that time, passing through the hands of Alice Dawson, nee Noble, and Veronica Ambler, nee Dawson, to the author. There is no record of the how the item was acquired, whether by purchase or by gift.[1]

SIGNIFICANCE

---
[1]   *Veronica Ambler in conversation with her family during her lifetime*

Commemorative items such as this are created as a reminder of events or occasions of significance. In England there is considerable interest in such events as royal births, weddings, coronations, deaths and significant visits. Purchase of such items is an expression of this interest.

This object is of particular significance as it commemorates two events that were of great importance to the people of Preston, Lancashire, in the north of England.

In 1179, King Henry II granted Preston the right to have a Guild Merchant. The Guild was an organisation of traders, craftsmen and merchants. Only members of the Guild could carry out a craft or business and newcomers could only trade with permission from the Guild. Anyone who claimed to be a member of the Guild had to swear loyalty to the Mayor and the Guild Merchant in a public court. Gatherings for renewing membership were only required once in a generation. From 1542, Preston Guild's renewal of membership, has taken place every 20 years (with the exception of 1942 due to WWII). Large numbers of people gather in Preston for the occasion, making the Guild festivities, including its grand procession, into a prestigious social occasion, and a tourist attraction.

Queen Victoria had reigned from 1837 until 1901. In the latter years of her reign many of her duties had been taken over by her son Albert Edward, Prince of Wales, and his wife Alexandra of Denmark. They had become very popular and England was anxious to see them on the throne. In 1902, a year after Victoria's death, England was ready to celebrate a new sovereign.

The Guild of 1902 coincided with the coronation of Edward VII and doubled the festivities of this highly anticipated Guild Year. Hence the creation of a Coronation/Preston Guild dual commemorative object.'The Guild has always been an important time in the lives of the members of the Dawson and Ambler families.

Preston Guild is a community expression of affiliations and identifications with work, education and religion. At each Guild since 1902 Amblers and Dawsons have participated in the processions as members of a trade, school or Church group.

As Councillor in the Preston Borough Council in 1902, Edward Ambler, Great Grandfather of the current Ambler generation, was a member of the Council leading the grand procession through the streets of Preston to the Guild renewal ceremony.

Many family memories are associated with the 1902 Guild commemorative cups. All revolving around the Guilds of 1902 - 2012 . The presence in the family of the objects is treasured as an expression of our family and town history. They have been used and brought out for tea as a 'special' cup and saucer for family visits. They have acted as a catalyst for conversation and the passing on of oral family history.

It is worth noting that this particular lithophane mould and pattern, were used as a commemorative item for the coronation of Edward and Alexandra throughout England. There were other towns that also adopted it as a dual commemorative or coronation gift to their citizens.'

Sources of information

Once you've dated the artefact, histories of that period can help give more on the historical context. If possible, finding other objects and sources that date from the same period and place can help you to generate the socio-cultural context.

Online access to museum collections can be vital in finding similar objects to compare with objects in your collection. They will help you to fill in the gaps in your visualisations of the how your family members and ancestors lived, the things they had and used in their homes and their culture.

Searching through collections can be challenging. You may end up with too many results or not enough!

Each online collection will have a different search function, but most will have options to customise or limit your search, and may allow you to have some control over how the results of your search are ordered.

Before you start to search, try to generate a list of possible keywords. Making a mind map can also encourage you to think of additional search terms.

Your description of your object will help you to generate a list of;

- materials
- functions
- place, maker and making techniques
- date or possible period of the object.

There are local museums and historical societies that have significant collections of everyday items, but do not have the financial or human resources to enable them to create online databases. Writing to or emailing these organisations, particularly those in the family's or ancestor's place of origin, with photographs of your object could result in someone being able to assist you with your research.

• •

THE FOLLOWING RESOURCES WILL BE OF ASSISTANCE IN IDENTIFYING AND DESCRIBING YOUR FAMILY OBJECTS.

1. Museum of Applied Arts & Sciences (Powerhouse Museum), Australia http://www.powerhousemuseum.com/collection

2. National Gallery of Australia http://nga.gov.au/Collections Te Papa Tongarewa Museum of New Zealand http://collections.tepapa.govt.nz The national museum of New Zealand, with a highly diverse collection.

3. Victoria & Albert Museum, United Kingdom (http://collections.vam.ac.uk/) Focus on art and design, including material from the colonies and other parts of the world as well as Britain.

4. Museum of London, United Kingdom https://www.museumoflondon.org.uk/collections As the name suggests, focused on London, with a strong collection of archaeological material.

5. Revolutionary Players of Industry and Innovation, United Kingdom http://www.revolutionaryplayers.org.uk Gathers material relating to the Industrial Revolution in the Midlands of the United Kingdom.

6. Ashmolean Museum of Art and Archaeology, United Kingdom http://www.ashmolean.org/collections Another diverse collection with a global scope.

7. Riello, Giorgio. 2009. Things That Shape History: Material Culture And Historical Narrative. In History And Material Culture.

8. Bullock, Veronica. 2009 Significance 2.0: A guide to assessing the significance of collections http://arts.gov.au/resources-publications/industry-reports/significance-20

9. Harvey, Karen. History and material culture: a students guide to approaching alternative sources. London: Routledge, 2009.

IMAGES AS ARTIFACTS

"The past can be seized only as an image which flashes up at the instant when it can be recognized and is never seen again."

Walter Benjamin

The things that are in a family collection inevitably include photographs, often in vast numbers, and possibly art works. Analysing these for their significance can be quite difficult, especially the art works.

For example, I have a pottery mask that was made for me by my niece when she was in primary school. Does it have significance? For me, yes, but for anyone else? Right now, probably not, but in the future when she has achieved prominence in her field, maybe. Time will tell.

There are many factors that need to be taken into consideration when deciding what to keep and what to discard. Not the least consideration is the question;

'Is it worth the effort I will put into creating its description?' If it is, then the image's basic characteristics are described.

Descriptions need to include;

- ೞ The medium in which it was created. Medium is the materials and related techniques used in making an artwork; for example, oils, watercolour, pastel, ink, print. Each of these has specific characteristics. Oil painting has particular strengths and limits: colour can be highly saturated, with an intense interplay of light and dark. Photography may not alway accurately reproduce colour, but it usually gives a clear, realistic sense of space and scale.
- ೞ The genre. The group within the general category to which the image belongs.
- ೞ In watercolour painting, this might be landscapes, portraits or miniatures, among others.

After that, it's the same process of placing it in the family context, making sure that the artist or the photographer is identified and described.

For example, on the right is an image description created to include in my father's records and the 'book of hand-me-downs'.

My father was an amateur artist. I have in my possession his first painting, and his last.

This image description is of the last of his paintings, created about 6 months prior to his death.

"PICNIC IN THE BUSH"

KENNETH EDWARD AMBLER - "PICNIC IN THE BUSH"   OIL ON CANVAS C.1994

This is a landscape in oils, created by Kenneth Ambler around 1994. It was the last painting created by Kenneth.

It is mounted in a timber frame, 410mm x475mm.

Currently in the possession of Mary Christine Sutton, his daughter.

Kenneth commenced painting in the late 1980s. He was inspired to take painting classes when his wife, Vera, who was undergoing treatment for breast cancer at the time, insisted he should 'have a go'. She believed it would give him something to focus on besides her illness.

Kenneth became an avid painter, showing the same creativity and ability to 'see' that he applied to his photography. He was very influenced by the artist Kevin Best. Best's ability to capture the light between the trees fascinated him. He tried to emulate this in all of his later paintings.

"Picnic in the Bush" was Kenneth's final painting. He believed it was the nearest he had been able to get to replicating Kevin Best's technique.

After Kenneth's death, Chris met Kevin Best at an exhibition and told him of her father's desire to 'get the light right'. The artist told her that this would not have been possible, as the secret to this technique was in the way in which he trimmed his brush.

Most of Kenneth's paintings are in the possession of family members. Christine has his first painting and this, the last painting he completed..

PHOTOGRAPHS

Paintings are probably not going to make up a huge percentage of your image collection. Photographs probably are.

The biggest decision you will have to make is which photos to keep and which to dispose of. Ask yourself the following questions;

- Who is in the photo? If the answer is 'I don't know', and no one else in the family can identify the people;
  - Ask the next question.
- Is it of a place special to the family? If the answer is 'no' or 'I don't know and neither does anyone else'.;
  - Ditch the photo.
- If you have answered with a name or place in the first two questions ask 'Is it unique? Is it special?" If the answer is 'yes';
  - Describe it, scan it, backup the digital copy and put the photo carefully away.

There are two types of photographs you will have in your collection, photographs of people and photographs of places.

Describe the photographs as fully as you can. Studio portraits should have the name of the studio/photographer recorded, if known.

Date the photo as closely as you can.

Place the photo in context.

- Who is in the photo?
- When was it taken?
- Was it taken on a special occasion?
- Where was it taken?
- Are there any particular features you need to point out?
- How did it come into your possession?
- If there are negatives, where are they stored? What condition are they in?
- How did the Photograph come into your possession?
- Who has the original?

PHOTOGRAPHS IN YOUR COLLECTION

STUDIO PHOTOGRAPHY

Photographic portraits in the nineteenth century were primarily confined to the studio. The studio gave photographers a controlled environment in which they could work. Here they could set up cumbersome equipment and handle delicate materials and time-sensitive processes. The controlled environment of the studio was also an aesthetically controlled space, with props and backdrops on hand to support the stylistic expectations of portraiture.

USING THE SURROUND: STUDIO BACKDROP AS DATING TOOL

'The surround' is a label for all the elements in the portrait apart from the person. In studio photograph, the surround can include the backdrop, props and furniture.

Studio backgrounds up to the 1860s were generally plain, with the subject seated.

In the 1870s, more sophisticated backgrounds and props had come into fashion, including columns, drapes and banisters. Furniture was usually heavily upholstered.

By the 1880s, the rustic look was very popular. In addition to backdrops pained as spectacular landscapes, props could include rough wooden fences and gates, grasses, and tree stumps.

In the 1890s and early decades of the twentieth century, cane furniture and rugs were common elements. Photographers did reuse props and furniture over long periods of time. The transitions between these fashions was not always made at the same time by all photographers, everywhere.

A good example are the three generations of professional Tasmanian photographers (Stephen Spurling I, II, and III) They show the potential longevity of photographic businesses.

OUTSIDE THE STUDIO

At the beginning of the twentieth century, the development of affordable cameras, and the ability to have someone else process the films, caused a shift in who took photographs, and where they were taken. Professional studio photographs continued, but the growth of amateur photography meant that more slices of daily life were being captured.

FAMILY PHOTOGRAPHS AND NATURAL ENVIRONMENTS

Decreasing size of cameras came at the same time as the growing popularity of the outdoors as a place for leisure activities.

In the 1920s and 1930s, car ownership grew and bush-walking became a respectable and popular leisure activity.

From this time, portraits place people at the centre of the image. Taking family photographs outdoors allows including people for scale, accentuating the landscape through small human figures.

Photographs can also embody a relationship to places. There was opportunity, too, to step away from portraiture, to compose the shot without any trace of human presence.

Landscape photography became an art form of its own from about the 1920s.

On the next page you will find an image description for a family photograph.

Kenneth Ambler is in the photo, together with his father, Edward, and brother Peter.

This photo is part of the same collection as the painting by Kenneth Ambler.

THREE GENERATIONS

EDWARD AMBLER

Black and white photo taken by Edward Ambler's friend S.W. Gee, C.1940

Original is negative only, scanned and inverted to digital form.

While the original was in a wallet of negatives that had belonged to Mr Gee, we can be reasonably confident that it was not taken on his camera, as he is holding his camera in his left hand in this photo. As he had a darkroom and was a keen photographer who processed all of his own work, we may assume that he developed the negatives for Mr Gee and stored them with his own.

There are visible marks of aging and deterioration of the negative coating, however the negative is in reasonable condition due to storage in an acid free, purpose made negative wallet.

The photograph shows from right to left;

- Edward Ambler
- Peter Gordon Ambler
- Kenneth Edward Ambler

The family home is in the background. As this was on Moor Park Ave, Preston, Lancs, UK it is entirely possible that the photograph was taken across the avenue in the park .

CARING FOR PHOTOGRAPHS

At this point it is useful to discuss how to care for all of those old photos that you have decided are important to keep. There are a number of types of common damage that different photographic materials experience; tears, losses, cracking of glass plates, lifting of emulsion, scratches, fading, discoloration, and colour shifting. In order to slow down or stop damage there are some things you can do.

One of the most important of these is handling. Make sure that things are flat and supported to prevent any sort of folding or tears or breakages. Make sure your hands are clean or, particularly when dealing with photographic prints, wear nitrile gloves so that you don't touch the emulsion and cause fingerprint damage.

Keep photographs in a stable environment if possible. Consider the light levels, relative humidity and temperature. The type of environment is very important. Photographs are particularly susceptible to light damage, so keep things in storage in the dark. Light damage is cumulative. Each time you expose a photograph to light, it will be adding to the age and deterioration. Scan once!

Light includes direct sunlight, UV is the most damaging to photographs, artificial light in rooms, including lamps and lights and LEDs. Minimise the amount of light exposure by keeping things in the dark but in that isn't possible limit the amount of illumination that you subject your photographs to by using low level LEDs and also the length of the illumination time that you subject them to. You may think about what blinds you have on windows to minimise the UV light that is coming into the room.

For very old photographic material types, such as daguerreotypes, expose it to light or keep it on display only for up to three months.

Look at the relative humidity and the temperature.

Within museums and art galleries the storage spaces use air conditioning and other systems, to keep environment as stable as possible. Within a home environment, if you try to keep it stable you are benefitting the preservation of the photographic material. Some of the things you can do is put dehumidifiers in a room. If it is particularly damp, you can use home air conditioning or heating systems. If you do have very high relative humidity, that causes things like mold outbreaks,it can be a catalyst for chemical change. A lot of photographs inherently deteriorate due to their processing and the chemicals that are used. If the chemicals have not been removed properly, damp and high relative humidity will act as a catalyst for this. Temperature is also a factor here. If you can, try to keep that stable as well. Aim around 20 degrees if possible within a display environment. It is beneficial to keep photographs in a colder cupboard or shelving as they don't mind being cooler in comparison to other object types.

If you want to display your photographs, there are a number of ways that preserve them, such as mounting them before framing. There are a number of different methods that you can use for mounting but as long as they're kept safe within the mount, then you're providing protection within the frame. Use a matte board at the front so that the photograph is not touching directly to the glass or perspex, whatever the glazing may be. It creates a bit of airflow. You want to avoid the photograph sticking to the glass at all costs by having the small spacer there, and having an enclosure within the frame that creates a micro environment with more stable relative humidity and temperature than the outside of the frame.

To minimise the light exposure to which you are subjecting the original materials, digitize it and display the copy. Keep the original in dark storage so that you're not destroying the original valuable item.

COLOUR PHOTOGRAPHS

Colour photographs come in different shapes and sizes, rounded corners, small squares, etc. Earlier photographs may be hand coloured.

It is preferable to keep colour photos in the plastic sleeves, but if you want to keep them in boxes, if you're stacking them on top of each other, or putting them on their edge within a box, you will have issues with abrasion, the back of one print rubs the front of another. Interleave them with acid free tissue.

Colour photography varies in the rates of deterioration. There have been many, many different types since its inception and the very early types may show colour shifting. This is most often seen on photos taken and processed from around the 70s.

 ↪ The prints may look blue or may look pink. This is because the colour has changed within the chemical process.

 ↪ You may also have colour photographs that are from the same negative within your collection but there is a difference between them. This is because one photograph was processed in the old analogue manner and the other processed digitally.

These days we're shooting digitally and we may go to the store and get them printed digitally.

You can see what type of print it is by looking at the back to see if there is any information on it.

Quite often you may have information about the type of paper that it has been printed on.

With the digital prints, it may have the type of digital paper or it may have a computer brand. That's a good clue that it is from a digital print.

These are more susceptible to fading and staining than a lot of the stable colour photography.

If possible, try to minimise the light exposure to these or ensure that you have the digital file so that you can reprint if for some reason it becomes damaged.

BACKUP! BACKUP! BACKUP YOUR PHOTOGRAPHS TO EXTERNAL MEDIA.

Always keep copies of digital photos and scanned photos in several places.

BLACK AND WHITE PHOTOGRAPHS

Black and white photography has many different formats. Early formats were small using black and white film and processed with black and white. Others are digital prints which look black and white but are actually colour printing materials which are mimicking black and white.

If you can identify that a photo is actually a colour photograph filtered to look black and white, follow the same recommendations as preserving colour prints by minimizing the light.

Traditional black and white photography is actually more stable.

However, with older photographs, you may find issues like an iridescence visible, silver mirroring, which occurs from silver gelatin prints.

Do not clean this off.

Even if it is obstructing an image. Do not try and clean the silver mirroring off yourself. When you remove the silvering, you're actually removing silver from the photograph and you may cause damage. It's preferable to send it to a conservator who can do it professionally and avoid damage.

A final word on protecting photographs.

Damage is often seen on precious photos from indentations on the photograph, ink and biro stains, where people have written on the back of the photograph, be wary of this.

Find another way to label them.

Wedding photo of Kenneth Edward Ambler and Veronica Dawson, taken April 1944. Photography by Edward Ambler, father of Kenneth.
Back row is the crew of Kenneth's Lancaster Bomber, shot down over Germany in the weeks after this photo was taken.
Of the seven airmen only 3 survived; Kenneth Ambler, Donald Harold Heggie, pilot, and Gerry Flanagan, navigator. Gerry was not on board the aircraft on that day.

STORING IMAGES AND ARTIFACTS

Displaying family objects allows you to see them regularly and to be reminded of their associated memories. It also enables the sharing of memories by creating discussion with other family members or visitors.

If you want to display or use objects from your family collection, these are the things you need to consider:

- ☙ Maintain a stable environment. Display and store objects in environments where changes in temperature and humidity are gradual (and where possible, minimal).
- ☙ Minimise exposure to light, especially the ultraviolet radiation in direct sunlight. Objects containing paper and textiles are the most vulnerable to light exposure, whereas ceramic and glass objects are not so sensitive.

  You may choose to limit exposure to light be keeping objects in darker areas of the house or only bringing them out for display for short periods of time.

- ☙ Support objects on display. Appropriate supports or enclosures for objects limit the potential for damage to the object during handling or while on display.
- ☙ Protect old china and glassware from dust, which may leach colours from hand-painted china. Resist the temptation to light the china cabinet. It creates heat and fades colours.
- ☙ Avoid placing cups upside down. This creates damage to the rim and rubs of any decorative or gilt trim.
- ☙ Do not store alcohol in crystal, it leaches the lead from the crystal and sends it cloudy - it also poisons the drinker! This is particularly so for antique crystal decanters.

Storing objects correctly enables you to keep them in an environment that minimises their exposure to light and fluctuations in their environment.

Starting at the level of the individual object, you need to assess the best conditions for that object.

Where objects are composite (made of more than one type of material) you need to prioritise the most vulnerable material within the object and suit the conditions to that.

There are numerous museum sites that offer advice on storing your treasures.

You may want to consider recording all of your treasures in a phone app that allows you to photograph each object and record a description.

These are stored in the cloud until you transcribe them.

One such app is *C3 - My Family Heirlooms*, which has versions for all types of phone and tablet.

STORING AND CONSERVING PHOTOGRAPHS

Preserving your photographs is particularly important in terms of storage. It's like Russian doll, one environment inside another until you get to the photo. So first, plan the enclosure that the photograph is actually kept in and there are a number of things that you can purchase either from archival specialists or from stationery stores or you can make your own. In Queensland the State Library is an agent for Albox. Albox is an Australian archival storage supplier. They carry products suitable for both images and objects at a reasonable price. Illustrations and prices below are from their online store.

You can get a range of materials that are specific for photographs and these include polypropylene sleeves. There are a number of different types that are specific to different photographic prints. They come in different sizes to house your negatives and transparencies. They can then be kept in a number of formats, such as folders, which are also made of polypropylene. Or you can purchase portfolios or folders which have a slip case and a ring binder style, so that the sleeves can easily be flipped through. Your stationer or photo shop will help you with these.

If you have things like glass plate negatives, you can buy small polypropylene folders. Within these you can stack the glass plates. It is important not to keep the actual plates face to face because the emulsions can rub against each other causing abrasion. Also, they may break if they're knocking against each other as glass is very fragile. Try to house things separately in four flat folders. Then it is easy to access the negative and it keeps them safe.

You may have lots of old negatives. Quite often people have kept these with a rubber band around the middle. Take that off! The rubber will deteriorate them and you will get indentations on your negatives. Old negatives may be housed in PVC which is not good for photographic materials. The polyvinyl-chloride will deteriorate and yellow them. It is preferable to take them out of these sorts of enclosures and use the plastic sleeves mentioned earlier.

Polypropylene sleeves for photographs and 35mm slides and negatives can be purchased online. There is a starter pack for family historians priced at around $30 available (November 2018) from the Albox online store. It contains;

- 1 x 40mm Binder and Slip Cover (acid-free)(320mm x 300mm with 40mm Spine)
- 10 x 6" x 4" pockets (acid-free)
- 5 x 9" x 12" pockets (acid-free)with (acid-free) white board insert
- 2 x 35mm negative pockets (6 strip) (acid-free)
- 1 tab sheet for recording information
- Available in Black, Charcoal, Oxford Blue and Light Grey
- Up to 33 more pockets can be added to this album.
- This particular folder again is a four-flat style and it's referred to as a Phase Box and the album is kept tightly within there and supported. It can then put on a shelf either flat, or like a book on the bookshelf.

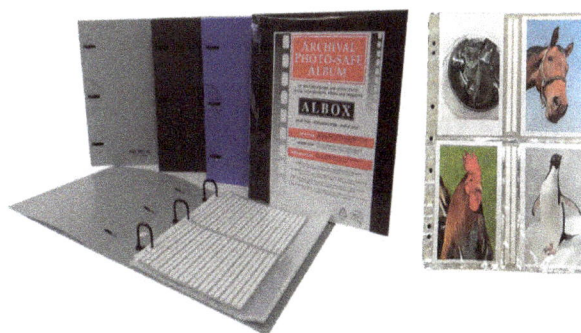

If you don't have money or time to buy proper archival materials, you can use other boxes and things around the house. However, things should be padded or supported so as to avoid damage or scratching.

If you have photographic albums, store them on shelves on open display or you can make custom made boxes. Use archival card which is acid free.

There are a number of plans and instructions online, that can be sourced from institutions such as the National Archives on how to make these.

There are different sized archival boxes, wallets and acid free inserts for boxes available for the storage of larger photographs, images and for objects.

For example, these 380mm(L) x 260mm(H) x 150mm(W) storage boxes are made from 1.0mm acid-free polypropylene. They;

- ℬ have inert box interiors
- ℬ are water & rodent resistant
- ℬ have an infinite lifespan
- ℬ are suitable for hot and humid conditions
- ℬ do not have internal finger holes
- ℬ are OHS&W compliant and
- ℬ have a spine label pocket

They cost about $10 each. A lining can be purchased for them to give extra protection from dust and humidity. Square and rectangular boxes are available in various sizes.

For larger photographs, maps or posters and fabric items, it's possible to acquire wallets and flat boxes.

There are wallets, boxes and folders for CDs and other audio items.

These come in the same materials as the boxes and board inserts can be purchased separately to give support to larger prints and maps.

There is an infinite variety of archival storage products to help you store and pass on your precious family treasures.

I suggest you explore following websites and download the Queensland State Library's *Guide to Selecting Preservation Material*, available free from their website. http://www.slq.qld.gov.au

- ℬ The Library Shop
  http://www.shop.slq.qld.gov.au/
- ℬ Albox http://www.albox.com.au/
- ℬ Archival survival
  http://www.archivalsurvival.com.au/

IF ALL ELSE FAILS...

If, despite all of your efforts to interest your children or grandchildren, you still find that no-one wants the family heirlooms, you have to decide what will happen to them.

There are some things you can consider;

- Talk to your extended family to see if there is another family historian in the next generation of cousins.
- Look for a local history museum or collector that would love to have them.
- Search for specialist museums and collectors.
- If they are rare and precious contact the State Museum.
- If they are military memorabilia speak to the Australian War Memorial.
- Speak to local antique dealers and sell them.
- Have an e-bay sale.

Whatever you decide, do it before it is too late, or make it clear in your will where these items are to go.

One thing is certain, if you have not organised your collection and its future, one day it will all end up on the dump!

CONSERVATION REFERENCES

1. Museum of Applied Arts & Sciences (Powerhouse Museum), Australia http://www.powerhousemuseum.com/collection Has a focus on Australian objects from design and industry contexts.

2. National Gallery of Australia http://nga.gov.au/Collections Fine and decorative arts collection that goes beyond Australia to include Pacific, Asian and European objects.

3. Te Papa Tongarewa Museum of New Zealand http://collections.tepapa.govt.nz The national museum of New Zealand, with a highly diverse collection.

4. Victoria & Albert Museum, United Kingdom (http://collections.vam.ac.uk/) Focus on art and design, including material from the colonies and other parts of the world as well as Britain.

5. Museum of London, United Kingdom https://www.museumoflondon.org.uk/collections As the name suggests, focused on London, with a strong collection of archaeological material.

6. Revolutionary Players of Industry and Innovation, United Kingdom http://www.revolutionaryplayers.org.uk Gathers material relating to the Industrial Revolution in the Midlands of the United Kingdom.

7. Ashmolean Museum of Art and Archaeology, United Kingdom *Collections Another diverse collection with a global scope.* http://www.ashmolean.org/

8. Riello, Giorgio. 2009. *Things That Shape History: Material Culture And Historical Narrative.* In History And Material Culture.

9. Bullock, Veronica. 2009 *Significance 2.0: A guide to assessing the significance of collections* http://arts.gov.au/resources-publications/industry-reports/significance-20

10. Harvey, Karen. *History and material culture: a students guide to approaching alternative sources.* London: Routledge, 2009.

11. Jayne Shrimpton's website *Family photos: what are they wearing?* http://www.jayneshrimpton.co.uk

12. The Conservation Centre, USA *The Importance of heirloom conservation* http://www.theconservationcenter.com/article/2716227-the-importance-of-heirloom-conservation

13. Roots Tech, Salt Lake City USA *How to Preserve Your Family Heirlooms* Video Members of the Conservation Team from the Church History Library and Church History Museum discuss general principles of preservation for your family heirlooms. https://www.rootstech.org/video/how-to-preserve-your-family-heirlooms

14. Jacobs, Deborah L. *When it's time to part with heirlooms and why I gave away Grandpa Oscar's violin.* https://www.forbes.com/sites/deborahljacobs/2014/03/31/when-its-time-to-part-with-family-heirlooms-and-why-i-gave-away-grandpa-oscars-violin/#22f75455ed8a

APPENDIX
FORMS, CHARTS AND LOGS

These are the standard Family History charts and research logs.

They support your research and document your sources.

You are free to copy these forms and use them to record your research findings.

They give integrity to your research and allow others to track where you have been.

They consist of;

1. Individual's Information Sheet - keep one sheet for each person in your family tree.

2. Four Generational Ancestral Chart - record four generations for a family starting with the closest to today on the left hand side.

3. Family Group Record - keep one for each couple and their children.

4. Research Extract - record each search and transcribe the findings.

5. Research Record - record each search and its results for a particular person.

6. Correspondence Record - keep track of who you have written to, or who has contacted you, in regard to your family research.

Individual's information sheet

NAME	Relation to you
Birth date/place	Death date/place

SPOUSE 1   **SPOUSE 2**

Name	....	....
Marriage date/place	....	....
Birth date/place	....	....
Death date/place	....	....

CHILDREN

Name	....	....	....	....
Birthplace	....	....	....	....
Name of spouse	....	....	....	....
	....	....	....	....
Marriage date/place	....	....	....	....
	....	....	....	....
Death date/place	....	....	....	....
Name	....	....	....	....
Birth date/place	....	....	....	....
Name of spouse	....	....	....	....
	....	....	....	....
Marriage date/place	....	....	....	....
	....	....	....	....
Death date/place	....	....	....	....

Occupation/s

Place of Abode (List each)

Notes

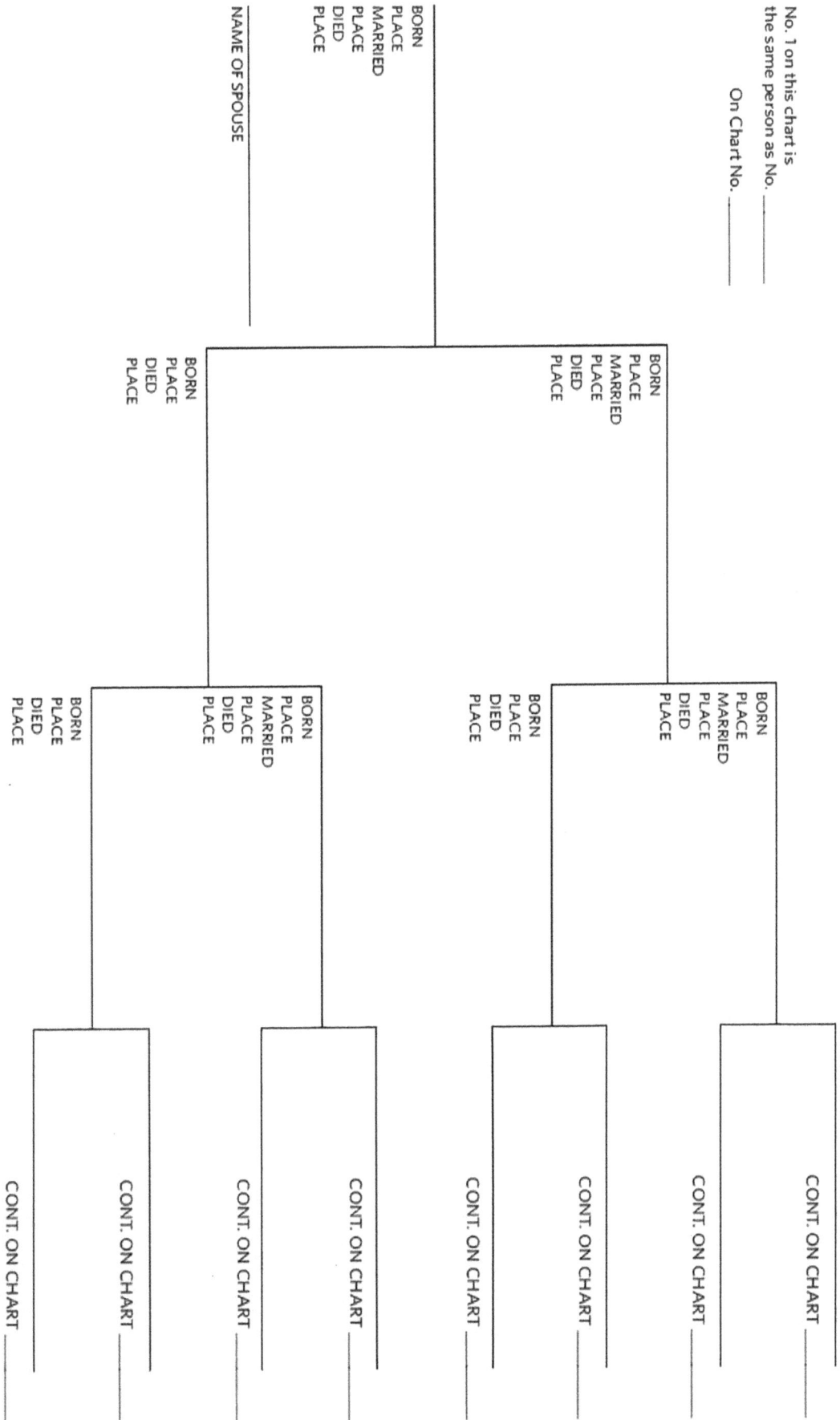

Ancestral Chart

No. 1 on this chart is
the same person as No. _____

On Chart No. _____

BORN
PLACE
MARRIED
PLACE
DIED
PLACE

NAME OF SPOUSE

BORN
PLACE
MARRIED
PLACE
DIED
PLACE

BORN
PLACE
DIED
PLACE

BORN
PLACE
MARRIED
PLACE
DIED
PLACE

BORN
PLACE
DIED
PLACE

BORN
PLACE
MARRIED
PLACE
DIED
PLACE

BORN
PLACE
DIED
PLACE

Chart No. _____

CONT. ON CHART _____

CONT. ON CHART _____

CONT. ON CHART _____

CONT. ON CHART _____

CONT. ON CHART _____

CONT. ON CHART _____

CONT. ON CHART _____

CONT. ON CHART _____

Family Group Record

Prepared By _____ Relationship to Preparer _____

Address _____ Date _____ Ancestral Chart # _____ Family Unit # _____

Husband

	Date—Day, Month, Year	Occupation(s)	City	County	State or Country	Religion
Born						
Christened						
Married						
Died						
Buried						Cem/Place				Name of Church
Father						Cause of Death
Mother						Other Wives				Date Will Written/Proved

Wife maiden name

		Occupation(s)				Religion
Born						
Christened						Name of Church
Died						Cause of Death
Buried						Cem/Place				Date Will Written/Probate
Father						Other Husbands
Mother						

•	Children Given Names	Birth			Birthplace			Date of first marriage/Place Name of Spouse	Date of Death/Cause			Computer I.D. #
Sex M/F		Day, Month, Year	City	County	St./Cnty	County	State/Country		City	County	State/Country	
1												
2												
3												
4												
5												
6												
7												
8												
9												
10												
11												
12												

Research Extract

FILE NUMBER/FAMILY		REPOSITORY	CALL #/ MICROFILM #
DESCRIPTION OF SOURCE			
INDEXED	CONDITION		DATE
TIME PERIOD/ NAMES SEARCHED			
SEARCH OBJECTIVE			

Research Record

Family _____ Researcher _____

DATE	REPOSITORY CALL #/ MICRO FILM #	DESCRIPTION OF SOURCE	TIME PERIOD/ NAMES SEARCHED	RESULTS

Correspondence Record

Family _____   Researcher _____

Date	To Whom	Purpose	Reply	Outcome

INDEX

For your own 'Scribbles'

www.ingramcontent.com/pod-product-compliance
Lightning Source LLC
Chambersburg PA
CBHW051611030426
42334CB00035B/3488